A Glimpse of
DARTMOOR

VILLAGES, FOLKLORE
TORS & PLACE NAMES

John Risdon
Andrew Stevens
Belinda Whitworth

**Peninsula
Press**

Published by Peninsula Press Ltd
P.O. Box 31
Newton Abbot
Devon TQ12 5XH

Tel: 0803 875875

A Glimpse of Dartmoor
Villages and Tors © Peninsula Press Ltd 1992
Folklore © Belinda Whitworth 1992
Place Names © Andrew Stevens 1992

Printed in England by D.D.S. Colour Printers, Weston-Super-Mare.

ISBN 1 872640 10 9

A GLIMPSE OF DARTMOOR

Contents

VILLAGES

FOLKLORE

TORS

PLACE NAMES

INDEX

St Pancras Church, Widecombe-in-the-Moor

A
Glimpse of
DARTMOOR

VILLAGES

John Risdon

**Peninsula
Press**

Photographs by the author.

The map of Dartmoor on pages 16-17 is reproduced with the kind
permission of the Dartmoor National Park Authority.

Published by Peninsula Press Ltd
P.O. Box 31
Newton Abbot
Devon TQ12 5XH

Tel: 0803 875875

© Peninsula Press Ltd 1992

Printed in England by D.D.S. Colour Printers, Weston-Super-Mare.

ISBN 1 872640 06 0

A GLIMPSE OF DARTMOOR
· VILLAGES ·

Contents

Introduction	5
Gidleigh	6
Holne	8
Lustleigh	10
Belstone	12
Postbridge	14
Map of Dartmoor	16
North Bovey	18
Lydford	20
Buckland-in-the-Moor	22
Poundsgate	24
Manaton	26
Sticklepath	28
Sheepstor	31

Buckland-in-the-Moor

Introduction

The following pages are intended as a brief introduction to twelve villages, or, in two instances, hamlets, that can be found within the Dartmoor National Park. It is a glimpse, a sample of what Dartmoor has to offer the visitor.

The villages cover a wide spectrum of Dartmoor's history and culture and all are unique in what they have to offer. Each one can be enjoyed at a glimpse, or, if preferred, delved into in greater depth. In either case finding the unexpected can give you the greatest satisfaction.

In the majority of cases Dartmoor's villages are of considerable age, and stone, timber and slate have weathered harmoniously into the surrounding landscape.

For those who wish to escape the multitude, commercialism and candyfloss for a while, these villages can offer a tranquillity and appreciation of all things beautiful, with man and nature working in harmony.

An additional bonus will be the country and moorland lanes with their vistas and hidden depths; lanes that have to be explored in order to reach the villages, as the majority are not on major highways.

To help you find your way, each village has an Ordnance Survey (O.S.) Landranger Map sheet number and map reference. All the villages can also be found on the O.S. Tourist Map of Dartmoor or the O.S. Leisure Map of Dartmoor.

In conclusion, may I wish you an enjoyable visit to the village(s) of your choice and PLEASE, may I respectfully remind you that every village, every house, every farm, is somebody's home; please treat it as though it was yours. THANK YOU on their behalf.

The Author

Born and bred in Devon, and with a career spanning the worlds of education and book-selling, John Risdon, has over 40 years, gained an intimate knowledge of an area which in his own words, has become part of his very being, developed through the soles of his feet, and the senses of sight, sound and feeling, together with the learned words of those like-minded Dartmoor folk that he has been lucky enough to spend time with.

◆

Gidleigh

Situation: O.S.Landranger Sheet No.191, map ref.671884
Services: Telephone box only.
Nearest town: Chagford.

In its isolated position, high up on the edge of the North Moor, the settlement of Gidleigh is rather more a hamlet than a village. Yet it is the centre of a widespread rural community. The less than half-a-dozen cottages that are situated near the little church of the Holy Trinity certainly define that fact. Also, in that the Post Office and Youth Hostel (shown on all O.S. maps) are no longer functioning at the time of writing, one could be misled into thinking that the community here no longer existed. However one would be wrong, and the use and upkeep of church and village hall indicate just how active is the wider community centred on Gidleigh. Look carefully and the signs are apparent, from the beautiful state of the interior of the 16th century church to the beech tree trunk notice board.

Beside the church are the remains of Gidleigh Castle. The castle was a fortified manor house in the 13th century, the medieval administrative and ecclesiastical centre of the whole parish of Gidleigh. Both church and castle are blanketed in a bed of rich tree growth and curtained behind lichen and fern covered walls.

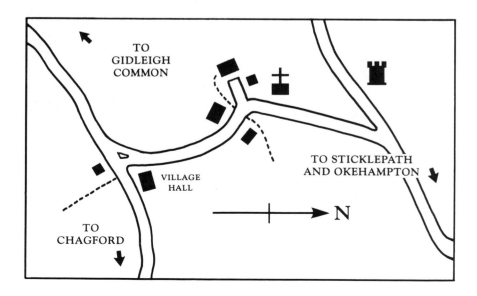

TO GIDLEIGH COMMON

TO STICKLEPATH AND OKEHAMPTON

VILLAGE HALL

TO CHAGFORD

N

Notice Board at Gidleigh

It is possible to visit this beautiful place and see no one. Peering through the ageing iron gates of the castle, it is easy to imagine that you are the first visitor for a hundred years.

Holne

Situation: O.S. Landranger Sheet 202, map ref. 7069
Services: Post Office/village store, pub, tea room.
Nearest town: Ashburton.

Holne village stands as one of the gateways to the moor, situated some 200 metres above sea level, on the very edge of open moorland. To the south the view is of the soft, rolling hills of South Devon; to the north, a descent to the deep, wooded valley of the Dart, as it drops rapidly from the moor. The name for this area and village has developed from the Saxon *holle*, meaning 'deep valley'.

Holne is a small and attractive village, little changed in physical size since medieval days. Its population has been intertwined with life on the moor since Saxon times with the land and tin mining being its main preoccupations. The Church of St Mary is, as in many villages, the central pivot of the community, and stands solid against the predictable south westerly gale. Associated with the church and village are two well-known men from the past. Charles Kingsley, author of such classics as *Westward Ho!* was born at the Rectory in 1819. More than one hundred years later, the then Archbishop of Canterbury, Michael Ramsey, returned year after year to take his holiday at Holne, a tranquil haven after the affairs of church and state.

The Church House Inn

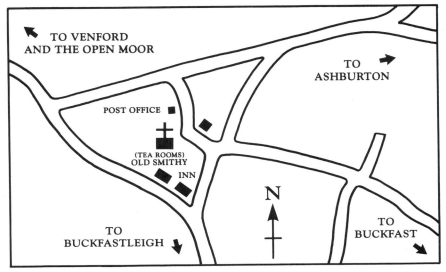

One can only wonder at how such men as these came to terms with certain village activities that were rather pagan in origin. For example 'The Holne Ram Feast' held in 'Play Field', saw the young men of the village catching the first ram they could find on the moor, and bringing it back to 'Play Field' where it was killed and roasted with great ceremony.

However, no doubt the power of both squire and vicar was considerable in days gone by; powerful enough to 'persuade' the blacksmith, being tempted every time he passed the Church House Inn on his way home, to take up new residence beside the smithy instead. (The smithy has since been converted into a charming tea room.)

As you enjoy a cream tea you can contemplate the fact that the same blacksmith, in addition to shoeing your horse, could also give you a quick haircut, thus making the most of his many skills, so necessary in an isolated community.

Should you leave the village on the Venford/Hexworthy road, as you drive through Moorgate out onto the open moor, spare a thought for the tin miners of Holne who had to trudge along this route, in all weathers, to the nearby mines. In the 1920's this particular piece of road was the first on Dartmoor to be tarmacked, bringing it well and truly into the 20th century.

Lustleigh

Situation: O.S. Landranger Sheet No. 191, map ref. 785814
Services: Post Office/store, dairy, tea rooms, select giftshop,
pub with accommodation.
Nearest town: Bovey Tracey.

The village of Lustleigh can be easily missed, lying as it does off the main Bovey Tracey/Moretonhampstead road, tucked in neatly amongst the foothills of Dartmoor. The name is probably better known in association with Lustleigh Cleave, a beauty spot situated to the west of the village.

The one drawback for the visitor, but one which has obviously helped to conserve the village's present identity, is a shortage of parking space.

The village has developed around the 13th century Church of St John the Baptist, which is in itself a building of considerable interest. Within the churchyard can be found another building worthy of attention - The Old Vestry. One presumes it was once used for this purpose but it was actually constructed in 1825 as the village school. Today it has a multitude of uses which reflect the active life of the village. The Parish Council hold their meetings here as do some of the fourteen local organisations, and it is also used as a surgery. Upstairs the village archives are lovingly cared for and added to by the local Historical Society. The exhibits are on view every Monday between 10 a.m. and midday.

The centre of the village has a cluster of 16th and 18th century buildings, including the village shops and pub. The village roots are indeed ancient and deep, with a mention in Doomsday as the only manor in Devon keeping bees for the production of honey; still obtainable today, throughout most of the year!

On the west side of the village, accessible down a cul-de-sac between dairy and Post Office, can be found 'The Town Orchard'. An area of 'semi-tamed land for the recreational use of the locals', it contains the granite throne, set up on a large granite boulder known as the 'Cleave' where the village May Queen is crowned on the first Saturday of that month.

In 1866 the opening of the Newton Abbot/Moretonhampstead railway line put Lustleigh on the map and made it very accessible to the Victorian day-tripper. Closed in 1958, the site of the old line still exists and seems to transect the village.

The village green, Lustleigh

In fact the settlement to the east of the line is called Wreyland, and was once a totally separate hamlet. It is a delight to walk along the footpath from Lustleigh green, passing under the old railway line and by the village cricket ground, to reach the picture-book thatched cottages of Wreyland, where the weathered skills of Victorian stone-masons, and the lack of car fumes contribute to a memorable experience. Wreyland was in fact the home of its own author, Cecil Torr, who wrote *Small Talk at Wreyland*, an insight into Devon village life with all its intrigues and gossip.

Radiating out from the village hub, Victorian, and later country residences, now cover the surrounding slopes, but with plenty of tree growth and 'sympathetic' gardening this later development blends in well.

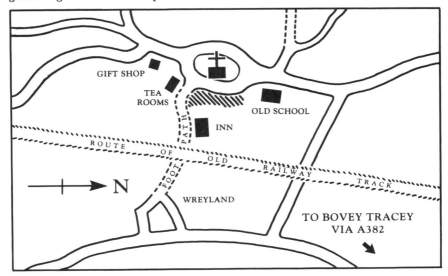

Belstone

Situation: O.S. Landranger Sheet No.191, map ref. 619936
Services: Post Office, licensed restaurant, smithy.
Nearest town: Okehampton.

The village of Belstone stands on the very flanks of the open moor, some 300 metres above sea level. It is very much a working village and not out to attract or depend on the sightseer, with the exception of the passing walker on his or her way on or off the moor, or riders on their way to the local stables.

In this hard environment the overall characteristic is one of resilience, with little to soften a rugged exterior. The buildings - including the Church of St Mary the Virgin - are low and squat, protection against frequent gales and rain.

Even so, its character has appeal, with some specific points of interest for the visitor. The most noteworthy and attractive is the Post Office, housed in what was once a Zionist Chapel built in 1841. It has been a Post Office, or, as stated above the door, a telegraph office, for at least 70 years.

Towards the bottom of the village, on the south side of the road, can be found the village stocks, complete with granite seat. Very thoughtful! Slightly further up the hill, on the same side of the road, is the village 'pound'. Constructed to keep stray stock in, it now contains a small garden, for the pleasure of all, and is well protected from the Dartmoor breezes.

The village stocks, Belstone

Old Chapel & Telegraph office, now Post Office

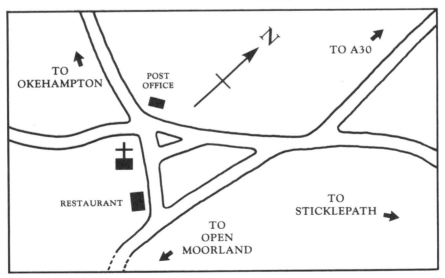

Postbridge

Situation: O.S. Landranger Sheet 191, map ref. 648790
Services: Post Office/village store/petrol pumps. Hotel/inn.
National Park Information Centre/Free Parking.
Excellent starting point for a range of walks.
Nearest town : Princetown.

Postbridge came into being to serve the Dartmoor traveller due to its stategic position as a crossing place over the East Dart. Originally a fording place, the developing trade in tin and wool during the 13th century saw a need to overcome the delays caused by the river when in flood and the now most visited 'clapper bridge' on Dartmoor was constructed. Forty-two feet long, by eight and a half feet high, constructed of four huge granite slabs supported on three piles, the bridge must have been of considerable benefit for the tinners and wool merchants en route between the stannary towns of Chagford and Tavistock.

As well as a river crossing Postbridge was a crossroads, with an important north/south track crossing the Chagford/Tavistock way here. However, it wasn't until the late 18th century that the village began to grow towards its present size and character. With the encouragement of the then Prince of Wales, together with people such as Thomas Tyrwhitt, areas of the moor were to be opened up to

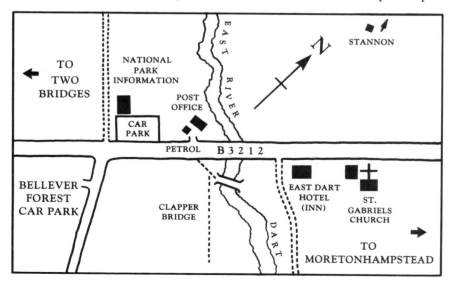

Postbridge(s)

both agricultural and industrial development. In the 1790's a turnpike road was built across the moor between Moretonhampstead and Tavistock with a new 'County' bridge - the present road bridge - built at Postbridge. A toll house and gate were positioned on the west side of the bridge, but these were demolished in 1863.

A new local industry launched in those pioneering days was the production of starch from locally grown cereals at nearby Stannon House. Many of the beech trees seen in and around the village were planted at this time. The present village hostelry, The East Dart Hotel, is a relatively modern building. Before its construction the village 'Ale House' stood just behind the present site. Further up the road, away from the bridge, can be found the small village Church of St Gabriel. Built in 1868 it was simultaneously used as both a chapel of rest and a day school! At the turn of the century children attending school had to bring one piece of peat each day to fuel the fire.

A final symbol of Postbridge's part in the Dartmoor scene is Drift Lane, the route off the North Moor, following beside the west bank of the East Dart into the village and easily viewed from the Tourist Information car park. Drift Lane was used for driving stock down off the high moor over many centuries, and now for the intrepid Dartmoor walker, the view of Postbridge must have been, and is, a welcome haven from what can be wild moorland weather.

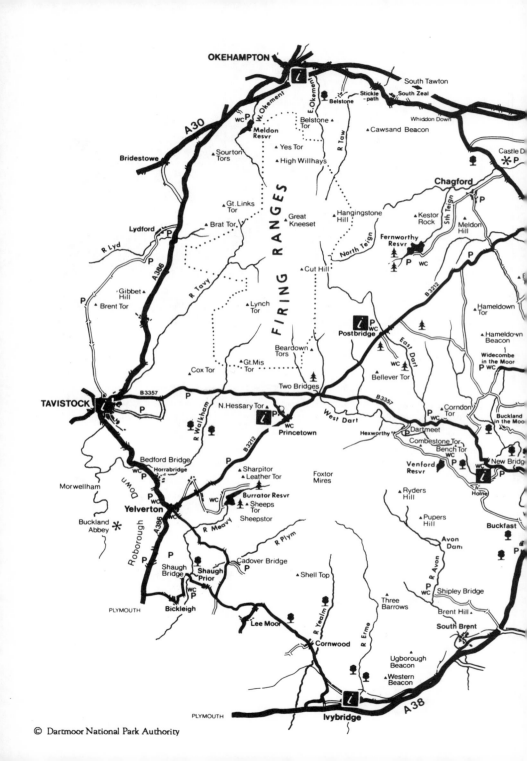

© Dartmoor National Park Authority

DARTMOOR

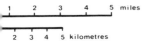

Map labels

EXETER

A30

ishop

nton

lge   R Teign

Dunsford
Steps Bridge
P WC
𝑖

B 3212

ardon
wn

Bridford

▲ Blackingstone Rock

etonhampstead

Christow

Kennick
Trenchford
& Tottiford
Resvrs
P

vey

Bovey
ton

Hennock

Lustleigh
Becky Falls

EXETER

or   HQ
𝑖   **Bovey
Tracey**

WC
P   Ilsington

A38

NEWTON ABBOT

NEWTON ABBOT

ASHBURTON

ASTLEIGH

S

OTNES & TORBAY

Key

KEY	𝑖	Dartmoor National Park Information Centre
	P Parking	**WC** Toilets

Scale

1	2	3	4	5 miles

2	3	4	5 kilometres

TO
ASHBURTON
12 MILES
MORETONHA
MPSTEAD
TAVISTOCK

North Bovey

Situation: O.S.Landranger Sheet 191, map ref. 740840
Services: Inn. Free car park opposite church.
Nearest town: Moretonhampstead.

North Bovey is one of those villages that, at first glance, seems frozen in time, except for the ever-present telephone cables and T.V. aerials. Situated around its village green the thatched cottages and church are a perfect example of 'the tranquil English village'. In fact, because it is situated in a backwater, on no specific route, it does not come to the attention of the majority of holiday visitors.

However, for those who like an uncommercial world for an hour or so it is well worth a visit. Pick your time well and the village pub, The Ring of Bells, whose structure and character merge perfectly into the village setting, will provide you with adequate refreshment. The Inn was originally a traditional Devonshire longhouse, with bakehouse attached and still visible.

The age of the majority of the village buildings is 15th and 16th century with the Church of St John the Baptist going back, in part, to the 13th century.
The population and services that once gave the village such a vigorous heart are now long gone. The fascination is in finding and mulling over the now-closed school house that had 65 children on roll only 30 years ago. Also the two village shops, now also sadly closed.

The village green is itself a place of fascination and interest. The present granite cross, although very old, replaced the original, destroyed during the Civil War. Also present are the village pump and a number of granite memorial stones celebrating such events as Queen Victoria's Jubilee. The chiming of the church clock as you look up towards the moor will complete a picture of a world now sadly past.

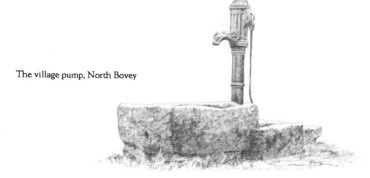

The village pump, North Bovey

The Church of St. John the Baptist, North Bovey

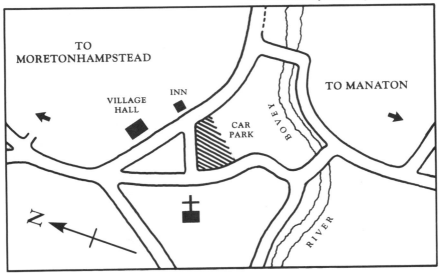

Lydford

Situation: O.S. Landranger Sheet No.191, map ref. 510848
Services: Post Office/shop, tea rooms, 2 pubs, garage, car park.
Nearest Town: Tavistock.

The village of Lydford has the honour of having been one of the four most important 'towns' in Devon. During the Saxon era, with the country experiencing attacks from the Danes, King Alfred made Lydford an administrative centre due to its good defensive site. With this function it was allowed to mint its own coins, samples of which can be seen in the Castle Arms Inn. Remains of the outer defensive bank can also still be seen running at right-angles away from the high street, just above (north-east) of the Post Office.

As time passed importance of one kind gave way to infamy of another. During the Middle Ages the tinners of Dartmoor were allowed to make their own laws and hold their own courts. This gave them considerable power over the local area and anyone involved in extracting tin. The original Norman castle at Lydford, built within the Saxon town area, was redeveloped as a prison for anyone breaking the tinners' laws. The present 'castle' is the ruin of that prison. From what we are told

Lydford Castle and the Castle Inn

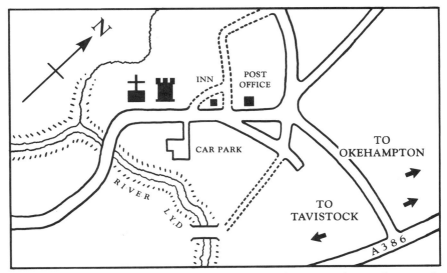

the innocent often paid the same price as the guilty, very often without trial. As the saying goes:

I oft have heard of Lydford law
How in the morn they hang and draw
And sit in judgement after.

Beside this gruesome place stands the 15th century Church of St Petrock, a beautiful and suitable counterweight to its evil but interesting neighbour.

In early medieval days the church at Lydford was the centre of a moorland parish of over 50,000 acres, and remains today the largest parish in Devon. In those early days anyone dying in the Parish had to be buried at Lydford. Across the moor there are various paths called 'Lich (or Lych) Ways'. These originated as routes for carrying the dead to Lydford for burial and were often of considerable length.

At the lower (south westerly) end of the village the hillside drops precipitously into Lydford Gorge and the River Lyd. It was this dramatic and beautiful natural feature that helped to make 'the town' such a defensible position in Saxon days. A walk along the gorge, now owned by the National Trust, is very worthwhile. Today Lydford is a small, sleepy Devonshire village, a long way removed from its Royal birth over one thousand years ago. Not for it the submergence under centuries of development, rather a bypassing of time, with a subtle wielding of influence over a moorland kingdom.

Buckland-in-the-Moor

Situation: O.S.Landranger Sheet 191, map ref.720730
Services: Craft shop/Tea rooms.
Nearest town: Ashburton.

A very small, picturesque village situated on the west facing, lower slopes of the moor, overlooking the Dart Valley and its tributary, the Webburn.

Although probably the site of a Saxon farmstead the name first appears in recorded form when Roger de Bokelonde gave the manor as a gift to the monks of Tor Abbey in the mid 13th century. This was in gratitude for his safe return from the Crusades. *Bokelonde* means 'the bookland' or land as detailed in a charter.

The village Church of St Peter, to be found at the top end of the village on the Widecombe road, is many centuries old with some original 12th century stonework still visible. It is a beautiful structure, its squat, grey granite form now as much a part of the landscape as the natural tors on the surrounding moors.

Today this church is probably best known for its unusual clock, to be found on the east side of the tower, facing the road. Instead of numbers there are letters making up the words 'MY DEAR MOTHER'. This clock face was donated in 1930 by William Whitley, the then 'Lord of the Manor', as a memorial to his mother.

Turning down beside the church is a steep, narrow, lane which leads the adventurous walker or driver into a woodland in which Grimm's characters would have felt at home. This lane and its surrounding beauty drops you quickly to the Dart and its confluence with the Webburn.

Should you ignore this route for the time being and continue on down the road towards the centre of the village you will pass Buckland Court on your right. This Georgian house was the family seat of the Bastard family, lords of the manor for many generations. The road, especially in summertime, seems to burrow

The tower of St Peter's Church, Buckland-in-the- Moor

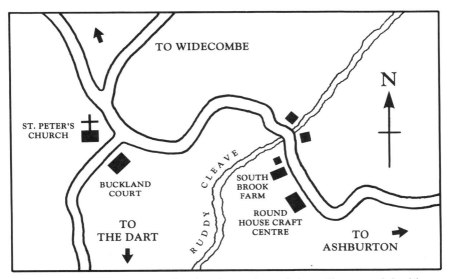

through luxurious vegetation, bordered on either side by walls covered thickly in moss and lichen. Set in this roadside wall, adjacent to Buckland Court, can be found an old medieval cross, if searched for diligently. The centre of the village consists of a cluster of granite and thatched cottages, together with what was once the school and the Post Office. They are situated on both sides of a fast-flowing brook, the Ruddycleave; no doubt named after the peaty colour of the water. Having filled a well-used horse trough, the stream passes under the road and on down the valley. This idyllic scene has graced many a chocolate box lid and the solitude, found more often out of season, appeals even to wintering herons who can be seen hunting for fish with enviable patience.

However, the scene is not always one of tranquillity. In 1939 the Ruddycleave brook became a destructive torrent and both cottage and bridge were carried away. Just up the road, on the opposite side, is Southbrook Farm, originally a manor court and of considerable importance to the local community. Adjoining the farm is the horse wheel barn, constructed in the last century to provide the farmer with an additional means of grinding corn. Today it has been converted into a craft centre and tearoom but it still retains the historical character of the area.

To the east of the village the hillside rises up onto the open moorland of Buckland Common. On the skyline, and visible from the church and other vantage points, you can see Buckland Beacon. Used as a signal point for centuries past, the Beacon, or tor, is well worth a visit, not only for the views that can be enjoyed from its summit, but also to inspect the 'Ten Commandments' cut into two slabs of granite in 1928 on the instruction of William Whitley.

Poundsgate

Situation: O.S. Landranger Sheet 191, map ref. 7072
Services: Post Office/village Store, pub, garage/petrol.
Nearest Town: Ashburton.

The village of Poundsgate could really be classified as a hamlet, yet it provides more for the local and visitor than many larger villages.

Like its neighbours Holne and Buckland, Poundsgate is set high up, 200 metres above sea level. It is impossible to miss the village as it is situated on either side of the main Ashburton/Two Bridges road, the A384. Although a major route across the moor, the narrow bridges across the Dart limit the amount of heavy traffic. After the steep climb up from New Bridge the village is a pleasant stopping place, especially on a sunny spring or autumn day.

The centre of the village, and the most conspicuous building, is the pub, the Tavistock Inn. Its most famous visitor is said to have been the devil, who called in with fiery breath to quench his thirst before continuing on his way to perform his destructive and deadly work at Widecombe on Sunday 21st October 1638. Today the Inn is a popular meeting place particularly during the summer months when it is renowned for its spectacular hanging baskets.

Further down the road towards Two Bridges, on the left, can be seen a traditionally constructed and picturesque granite cottage. Recently renovated, this building is thought to be originally 17th century, and was once the Post Office, complete with original telephone exchange for the Spitchwick/Holne area. Next door was once the village bakery and opposite was the smithy, with the mounting block still in place at the side of the building.

As you climb out of the village around a steep, tight hairpin bend, a small 'pound' or enclosure can be seen at the side of the road, on the left. This is the pound which has given the village its name. Used for enclosing stray stock, it still has some use today.

Further on up the hill and then to the right, can be found Leusdon Church. Set in glorious isolation, overlooking the Webburn and Dart, this small country church serves Poundsgate and the other hamlets and farmsteads of Spitchwick.

The Tavistock Inn

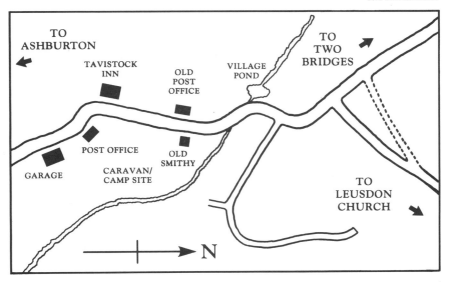

Manaton

Situation: O.S. Landranger Sheet 191, map ref. 750813
Services: Post Office/village stores. pub.
Nearest Town: Moretonhamstead.

Manaton village is the centre of one of Dartmoor's largest parishes and the village, although sparsely populated, is spread over a considerable area. It is, in fact, divided into three parts, all lying off the B3344 Bovey Tracey road. The original village centre nestles beside its 15th century mother Church of St Winifred, with village green and separate village cricket pitch in close proximity.

A third of a mile down the road towards Bovey are the other two parts of the village, once the evocatively named, independent hamlets of Freeland and Water, now all part of Manaton. As one drives along the road, the Post Office and Kestor Inn (headquarters of the M.C.C!) are clearly seen, but the more picturesque parts

Water, Manaton

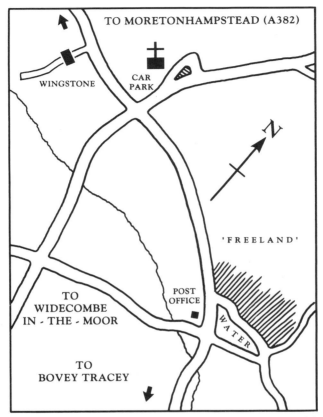

of Freeland and Water are not. A brief stop here, and time to amble along the narrow lane to the east of the road, enables you to experience a combination of weathered thatched cottages set in granite, lush vegetation and dancing water; a harmonious blend of man and nature. Water, as you might imagine, is the ideal site for a mill and indeed, there it still stands, but now a private residence.

The stimulation of the beautiful surroundings and the local populace were obviously an important factor in encouraging the poet John Galsworthy to make his home here at 'Wingstone', close by the church.

Ponder awhile and no doubt you will understand why.

Sticklepath

Situation: O.S. Landranger Sheet No.191, map ref. 640940
Services: Post Office, village store, 2 inns, garage/car hire.
Nearest Town: Okehampton.

The village of Sticklepath owes its existence to its position on what was once a major trade route between Exeter and Launceston, and to trades associated with the industrial revolution. As such, its background, buildings and character are not dissimilar to certain villages in the Midlands and South Wales, although of course those industrial days are long gone.

Up to the mid 1980's, Sticklepath's life was inextricably bound to the main Exeter/Okehampton trunk road - the dreaded A30 - with heavy traffic thundering incessantly through the village. But the construction of the new dual-carriageway has meant that, for the first time in its existence, the village has become a backwater, no longer on a main artery of commercial life.

Three hundred years ago the A30 was no more than a track, but it brought life to the area. It was along this track, where it fell steeply down the hillside to the River Taw, that the village developed. 'Stickle' in fact means 'steep' and referred to the steep track descending, or climbing,'The Mount' before the present road was built taking a more gentle route. The Mount is the conspicuous hill at the western (Okehampton) end of the village.

Although a small hamlet was probably here in Saxon and Norman times, it was the industrial revolution and the need for a source of power, close at hand, that saw Sticklepath blossom. Water from the River Taw, pouring off the moor, was to turn at least seven water wheels and thereby drive a multitude of machines, from bellows to hammers. A leat was taken from the river at the base of The Mount, along the backs of the various mills and works, parallel with the main street, and then back into the river.

During the 18th and 19th centuries, Sticklepath's proximity to the tin and copper mines of Devon and Cornwall, and the local copper mines of Ramsley and Greenhill, provided a ready market for a whole range of mining equipment.

Today, a part living reminder of the past industry of this little place can be seen and experienced in the Finch Foundry Museum. The original foundry, complete

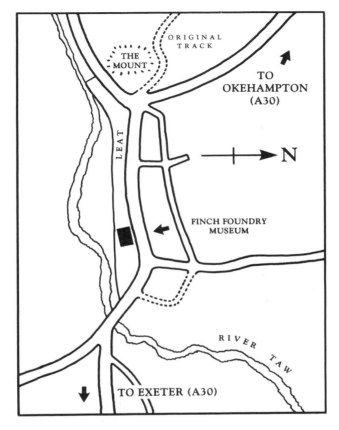

with water wheel, launders and working machinery, remains in being and is currently being renovated to give an accurate example of the power of water and the skills of our predecessors.

The people who had settled and made their homes in Sticklepath had much in common with other similar mining and industrial communities. The road very much played its part in bringing strangers, views and news at a time when communications were often lacking. It was the road that brought the Quaker religion to Sticklepath during the reign of Charles II, with the influx of a Quaker community of 200 people. A century later it was the road that brought John Wesley through the village. It is said that in response to local demand, he preached to the villagers on The Mount, where a white flagpole now stands. From then on the local community became very much a Methodist stronghold.

Sticklepath is also a well known name in geological circles as one of the longest fault lines in the West Country runs through the village and is named after it. Over millions of years the land has moved in opposite directions along either side of the fault. How many of the millions of travellers who have passed along this road will have known that the ground that contains the old mine workings at Ramsley, and that at Greenhill, were once adjoining? Today they are one mile apart!

Who would have thought that such examples of power and movement, both physical and spiritual, could be found in what is now such a peaceful backwater?

The now tranquil high street of Sticklepath, once the main route from Exeter to North Devon

Sheepstor

Situation: O.S.Landranger Sheet No.202, map ref. 560677
Services: None.
Nearest Town: Yelverton.

Sheepstor is another small Dartmoor settlement serving a population over a large area, although much of that area now lies under the waters of the Burrator Reservoir. Before the building of the reservoir, which supplies Plymouth, the area was much involved with mining and agriculture.

For the people living within this parish, the church at Sheepstor was where they would come on a regular basis. The hamlet - which takes its name from the mighty tor standing protectively to the north - seems to be an extension of the same natural phenomenon, with its narrow lanes, lichen-covered and granite-lined, and the church itself, spilling to the valley floor to lie exposed to the elements, without the dressing of abundant foliage usually found in similar settings.

The church and its surrounding cottages, clustered tightly together, provide a peaceful haven from the seasonal bustle beside the Burrator dam. This tranquil church is an apt resting place for two members of the Brooke family, once owners of a local estate, as well as being 'Rajahs of Sarawak' during the 19th and early 20th

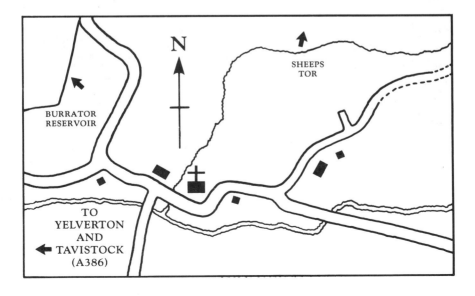

centuries. Inside the church there is a large commemorative plaque which describes in detail the long-term unselfish service the family gave to Sarawak and its people, all those thousands of miles away.

Sheepstor village

A
Glimpse of
DARTMOOR
FOLKLORE

Belinda Whitworth

Peninsula
Press

The map of Dartmoor on pages 16-17 is reproduced with the kind permission of the Dartmoor National Park Authority.

Illustrations by Brian Ainsworth.

Published by Peninsula Press Ltd
P.O. Box 31
Newton Abbot
Devon TQ12 5XH

Tel: 0803 875875

Printed in England by D.D.S. Colour Printers, Weston-Super-Mare.

ISBN 1 872640 08 7

A GLIMPSE OF DARTMOOR
· FOLKLORE ·

Contents

Introduction 4

GHOSTS 5

The Hairy Hands 6

The White Bird of the
Oxenhams 6

Lady Howard of Fitzford 7

Ponies, Pigs, Goats
and Dogs 8

WITCHES 10

Witches and Hares 11

Vixana 11

Witchcraft Yesterday
and Today 12

PIXIES 13

The Tulip Pixies 14

The Magic Ointment 14

Habits and Haunts 15

MAP OF DARTMOOR 16

PEOPLE AND PLACES 19

The Nine Maidens 20

Crazywell Pool 21

Jay's Grave, Childe's
Tomb and Fitz's Wells 22

Lydford 23

Spinsters' Rock 24

Bowerman's Nose 24

The Dewerstone 25

SAYINGS AND
SUPERSTITIONS 26

CALENDAR 28

BOOKS 32

Introduction

With its lonely uplands, isolated homesteads, windswept rocks and chattering streams, Dartmoor has been described as the last wilderness in southern Britain. Its rich history goes back to earliest times, with evidence of prehistoric, Celtic, Saxon, medieval and later settlement.

Its folklore is equally extraordinary.

In the following pages you will find malicious and mysterious pixies, Dewer the ferocious huntsman with his eerie Wisht Hounds, 'hairy hands', rocks that dance, pools that speak, witches and phantoms, charms, omens and superstitions.

If this whets your appetite for more, then as well as visiting the area for yourself and meeting its inhabitants you might like to look at some of the books on page 32 or even consult classic Victorian texts by Dartmoor's first folklorists such as the Reverend Sabine Baring-Gould, William Crossing and Mrs Bray.

The maps referred to in this book are: Ordnance Survey Outdoor Leisure: Dartmoor (2½ in to 1 mile) - Ordnance Survey Landranger 191: Okehampton and North Dartmoor (1¼ in to 1 mile) - Ordnance Survey Landranger 202: Torbay and South Dartmoor (1¼ in to 1 mile). In the text the numbers of the last two maps precede relevant map references to show on which of the two maps you will find a particular place, e.g. 'the Nine Maidens (191/614928)' means that you will find the Nine Maidens on Landranger map 191 and the grid reference is 614928.

The Author

Belinda Whitworth has lived in Devon since 1976. A freelance book editor and writer, she is also the author of *Gothick Devon* (Shire 1993). She is a member of several different local, national and international environmental organisations.

◆

Ghosts

The Hairy Hands

This macabre story is unique to Dartmoor and unusual in that all the events took place this century, in the 1920s, although similar legends have been in existence in the area for a very long time.

On an innocuous-looking stretch of the B3212 at Bellever Forest (191/646788 to 635771) between Postbridge and Two Bridges a series of inexplicable and sometimes fatal accidents began. Carts overturned, bicycles went out of control, horses shied and cars skidded. Finally, an army despatch rider, after a motorcycle crash, told of a pair of hairy hands that had seized the handlebars and wrenched his bike off the road.

By this time, the authorities decided to do something, and the camber of the road was altered.

A few years later on a moonlit night in a caravan near the same spot a woman awoke to see a large hairy hand clawing at the window. In her terror she made a sign of the cross, and the hand vanished.

One explanation of the hands is that they belong to an 'elemental', a semi-formless being, or to a crash victim haunting the area. Another, that they are echoes of past violence - the area was thickly populated in the Bronze Age.

Whatever they are, they seem now to have gone to ground ... or have they?

The White Bird of the Oxenhams

Many of Dartmoor's ghost stories are obviously the results of overactive imaginations or the reworking of stereotypes. This chilling legend is one of the few that seems to have suffered little in the way of distortion or embellishment since its origins, and is truly mysterious.

The Oxenhams came to Dartmoor in the sixteenth century. Oxenham Manor (191/665943), now much altered, is in South Tawton, on the northern edge of the moor.

There was a tradition going back to the early middle ages that the death of one of the family was heralded by a white or white-breasted bird.

The most famous incident concerns 'Lady' Margaret Oxenham. At a feast on her wedding eve her father saw a white bird hovering over her head. The next day in the church a rejected suitor stabbed her to death.

There are reliable written accounts of sightings from the seventeenth century onwards. Among them is one in the British Museum and the Bodleian Library at Oxford dated 1641. This refers to four members of the family who died and says that witnesses to the appearance of the bird 'were not by any rewards hired to speak so' and were examined for the truth of their testimony by a minister.

The last written evidence describes the death of an Oxenham in 1873 when the bird was seen by someone who had no knowledge of the tradition. Finally, just before the First World War, neighbours of an Amyas Oxenham who was living in Exeter say they saw a white dove fly in through his bedroom window shortly before his death. Amyas's son went to live in Canada and there are even reports that the bird was seen across the Atlantic.

The direct family line is now extinct.

Lady Howard of Fitzford

> My Ladye hath a sable coach
> With horses two and four
> My Ladye hath a gaunt blood-hound
> That goeth on before.
> My Ladye's coach hath nodding plumes
> The driver hath no head.
> My Ladye is an ashen white
> As one that long is dead.

A more baroque story this time, and perhaps less credible. Because of supposed crimes during her lifetime, Lady Howard's ghost is condemned to travel every night from Fitzford House in Tavistock to Okehampton Castle (191/585942) on the King's Way moorland track via Lydford. At Okehampton the dog must pluck a blade of grass and take it back home and only when all the grass has been removed from the castle's grounds can the lady rest in peace.

In some versions of the story Lady Howard rides in the coach, in others she is herself the 'gaunt blood-hound', a black creature sometimes with one eye and sometimes with two. The story doesn't specify why the driver should be headless.

The legend probably refers to a seventeenth-century Lady Mary Howard. However, although her father was apparently extremely dissolute and responsible for at least two murders, she herself was not evil, just forceful. It is possible that she has been confused with a Lady Frances Howard at the court of James I who was sent to the Tower for poisoning two of her four husbands.

There is a Lady Howard's Walk in the grounds of Okehampton Castle and the gateway of Fitzford House still stands. The poem is part of a ballad recorded by the folklorist the Reverend Sabine Baring-Gould (in *Songs of the West*) at the turn of the century.

▨ *Ponies, Pigs, Goats and Dogs* ▨

Wild ponies have ranged across the moor since prehistoric times but phantom ponies do not seem to have appeared much before this century.

On Gidleigh Tor (191/672878) during the Second World War the sound of hooves thudded close by two members of the Home Guard but no animal ever materialized.

In the 1960s a group of ponies was heard on Petticoat Lane leading into Throwleigh (191/667908) and a rush of wind was felt, but again nothing was seen.

A motorist drove straight through a pony in Hart Hole Lane going down to Dartmeet. The animal vanished into thin air and the car was undamaged.

An old and rather sad tale is that of the phantom sow and her starving litter who travel fruitlessly in search of food between Merripit Hill (191/658803) and Cator (191/680760).

A headless goat was seen in the 1930s in the lane leading to Wallabrook Bridge (191/653871) and one has also been seen several times near Postbridge.

If there is any connection between these goats and the animal sacrifice probably used by the moor's early inhabitants then this distressing apparition may have originated thousands of years ago.

Stories of ghostly black dogs, and packs of hounds in particular, are found all over Europe and Dartmoor is no exception. Here they are called the Wish, Wist or Wisht ('wisht' being an old word for eerie), Yeth or Heath Hounds and frequent in particular Wistman's Wood and the Dewerstone (SX538639) (see also page 25).

Other mystery dogs have been seen on the B3212 between Moretonhampstead and Postbridge and between Princetown and Plymouth, at Okehampton Castle (191/585942) - perhaps this is Lady Howard's ghost (see page 7), above Pizwell (191/669785) and at many other places all over the moor. A white dog has been seen on Cator Common (191/670770).

Probably the most famous of these creatures is the fictional 'hound of the Baskervilles'. Conan Doyle used to stay near Buckfastleigh and no doubt heard the story of the town's Squire Cabell who was so wicked that when he was buried the Wisht Hounds came to howl at his tomb. Grimpen Mire in *The Hound of the Baskervilles* is thought to be based on the treacherous Foxtor Mires (202/610700).

Witches

Witches and Hares

Witches are supposed to be able to change form and there are several Dartmoor stories, mostly rather nasty, about witches turning into hares. The following is a typical example.

A poor old woman heard that a local hunt was offering sixpence to anyone who could put up a hare for them. She told her grandson that she would predict where a hare was to be found and he must then tell the hunt.

In this way the old woman managed to earn several sixpences, but the hare was never caught, and the hunt began to get suspicious. One day after they managed to wound the hare they followed it into the old woman's cottage where it had fled. Inside they found no hare but instead the old woman in bed, dressing a large wound in her leg, in exactly the same place as the hare's wound had been.

This time they had no proof but later, for bewitching a young woman and making her spit pins, the old woman was burnt at the stake.

Hares have long had supernatural associations. Along with black dogs, they are supposed to haunt three-way crossroads, a particular feature of Devon and Dartmoor. A symbol consisting of three hares or rabbits in a circle was used by the moor's tinners and decorates the roofs of some of the moor's churches, such as Widecombe and North Bovey.

Vixana

Vixana was a witch who lived on Vixen Tor. She used to enjoy luring travellers to their death in the bogs which then surrounded the tor by calling down mists to confuse them. One day a man who had been given a ring by the pixies to make him invisible and who could see through mists crept up behind her and pushed her off the rocks to her death.

Vixen Tor (191/542743) is near the B3357 between Tavistock and Two Bridges, and there is a footpath from Merrivale. From the road the tor looks like a man and woman on horseback but from nearer to it looks like the head of an old woman.

Witchcraft Yesterday and Today

Charm for burns

Three Angels came from North, East and West
One brought fire, another brought frost
And the third brought the Holy Ghost.
So out fire and in frost.
In the name of the Father, Son and Holy Ghost.

Some say witchcraft is derived from ancient pagan religions whose followers, men as well as women, worshipped nature, particularly the sun and moon, and practised crop fertility rites.

It is possible that Dartmoor's standing stones were used in some of these early rituals. Charcoal has been found in the centre of some of the larger circles, suggesting that they were used for ceremonial fires.

Sheep sacrifice was practised on the moor until last century and ram-roasting festivals were carried out at menhirs (single standing stones). These may have been some of the last public demonstrations of the 'old religion'.

If witchcraft did exist, it must have been forced underground by Christianity, but its practices would have lingered in out-of-the-way places like Dartmoor. Some of the legends attached to the moor's prehistoric remains, such as the Nine Maidens (see page 20), may point to these unorthodox religious activities.

Right up until this century Dartmoor had a strong tradition of charms and curses, many of them, like the one above (from *Folk Rhymes of Devon* by William Crossing), a fascinating mixture of 'superstition' and Christianity. Not long ago a large coil of human hair was found in a cist (a stone tomb) on the moor, proof perhaps of even more recent activity.

Pixies

There's piskies up to Dartymoor
And t'idden gude yu sez there b'aint.

Just as Ireland has its leprechauns and Scandinavia its trolls, so Dartmoor has its pixies.

There are innumerable stories about them. 'The Tulip Pixies' is one of the most charming, whereas 'The Magic Ointment' illustrates the darker side of the pixy character.

The Tulip Pixies

Not far from Tavistock on the edge of the moor was a cottage with a pretty garden full of flowers. At night the woman who lived there would wake to the sound of sweet music, and the tulips she had planted gave off a scent more lovely than that of honeysuckle or roses.

The ability to see pixies is given to few but one evening at dusk as the woman looked out of her window she saw pixies bringing their babies and laying them each in a tulip flower to sleep. The woman realized that it was the pixies' breath that was scenting the flowers and the music was the lullabies they sang.

When the woman died the cottage was bought by a man who uprooted all the flowers so that he could plant vegetables. The pixies were heartbroken and left the garden, never to return. Soon it was a desolate waste as nothing would grow there any more.

With loving care the pixies tended the woman's grave instead, making sure that the turf was always neat and green and that beautiful flowers grew there all year round.

No one ever saw them but sometimes at night people would hear sad singing and know that it was the pixies mourning their departed friend.

There is a modern sequel to this story in Kitty Jay's Grave (see page 22) where a mystery pot of flowers is always found.

The Magic Ointment

One stormy night a Tavistock midwife was woken by a violent banging on her door. On her doorstep she found an ugly little man holding a large black horse with eyes of fire.

"Come quickly", he said, "My wife needs your help."

Reluctantly she mounted the horse behind the man and allowed herself to be blindfolded.

Eventually they arrived at a cottage and the midwife assisted at the birth of the woman's baby. The mother asked the midwife to rub some ointment on the baby's eyes. Out of curiosity the midwife then secretly rubbed some on one of her own eyes. Instantly the mother was transformed into a beautiful fairy-like lady and the baby was wrapped in silver gauze.

The next day as she went to market she saw the little man again and went up to speak to him. He was astonished that she could see him and asked which eye it was that she saw him with. He then struck the offending eye and caused her to be blind in that eye for the rest of her life.

In another version of the story a Holne midwife takes the ointment home with her by mistake and there tries some on one of her eyes. This time it makes everything seem larger than normal, but unnaturally clear, with the stars shining even though it's daytime. Unhappily the conclusion is the same.

Habits and Haunts

Although they can be kind, pixies are more often mischievous, even malicious. They are almost always secretive.

Sometimes they are dressed in rags, sometimes in colourful doublet and hose. Sometimes they are slim and fairy like, sometimes like miniature wizened people.

Some of them help about the house and people leave bowls of milk or water out for them. Others take horses by night and return them in the morning, lathered and exhausted. Some even steal children.

But their favourite activity is dancing and you can often see the circles of extra-green grass they leave behind.

To be 'pixy-led' is to lose your way and become confused, like John Fitz (see page 23). One of the few remedies is to turn your coat or your pockets inside out as quickly as possible.

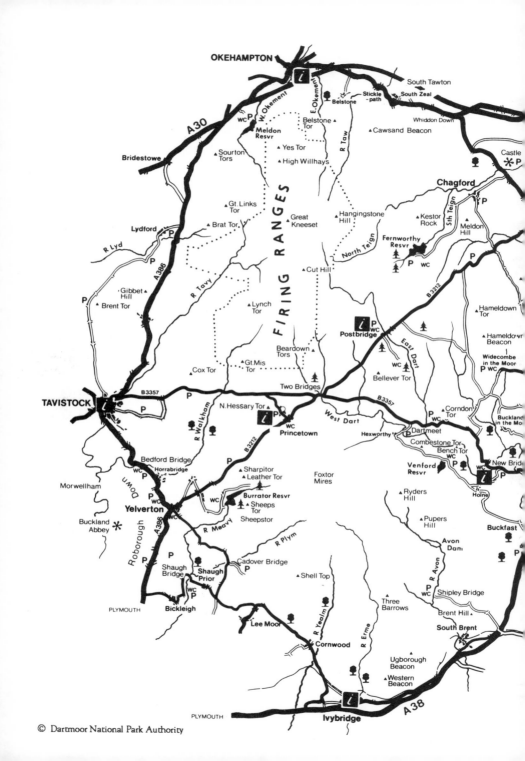

© Dartmoor National Park Authority

DARTMOOR

Bishop

EXETER

A30

gnton

dge

R Telgn

Dunsford
Steps Bridge

P WC

B.3212

Mardon
Down

Bridford

▲ Blackingstone Rock

retonhampstead

Christow

Bovey

R Bovey

Kennick
Trenchford
& Tottiford
Resvrs

P

aton

Hennock

Lustleigh

Becky Falls

P

Tor

EXETER

HQ

**Bovey
Tracey**

or

WC

P

Ilsington

on

A38

NEWTON ABBOT

NEWTON ABBOT

ASHBURTON

bey

FASTLEIGH

NES

n

TOTNES & TORBAY

| 1 | 2 | 3 | 4 | 5 miles |

| 1 | 2 | 3 | 4 | 5 kilometres |

As well as grassy swards, pixies also use the moor's prehistoric stone circles for their revels and many other places have special associations with the 'little people'.

New Bridge (202/712708) - a picturesque medieval bridge between Holne and Holne Chase where pixy revels have been heard at night.

Pixies' Cave or House (202/567681) - a narrow granite cave below Sheepstor (202/566682), used by Cavalier fugitives during the Civil War.

Pixies' Cross (191/534742) - one of the moor's ancient stone crosses, over seven foot high.

Pixies' Holt (191/668733) - a rock passage some four feet wide and thirty-seven feet long near Dartmeet, 'holt' meaning a hollow.

Pixies' Parlour - a tumble of boulders on the footpath between Fingle Bridge (191/743899) and Sandy Park (191/712896) where pixies meet and dance.

The Puggie Stone - an enormous boulder on the banks of the River Teign near Holystreet (191/688878) with a strong tradition as a pixy meeting-place; the name is related to Puck, the arch-pixy.

There are documented sightings of pixies right up to the present day but it has been suggested that legends about pixies and similar beings are folk memories of actual races that disappeared or were driven by invaders to remote woods and caves.

Some archaeologists believe that there was an early type of human being even smaller than pygmies. Dartmoor itself has been inhabited since the Stone Age by successive groups of people including bronze-users and Saxons, and possibly Celts as well.

People
and Places

The Nine Maidens
(191/614928)

And now at every Hunters Moon
That haggard cirque of stones so still
Awakens to immortal thrill,
And seven small maids in silver shoon
'Twixt dark of night and white of day
Twinkle upon the sere old heath
Like living blossoms in a wreath,
Then shrink again to granite grey.

There are two versions of the delightful legend attached to this group of standing stones on Belstone Common.

The more usual belief is that the stones dance every day at noon. In his poem above (from *Book of Avis*) Eden Phillpotts, the Dartmoor novelist, describes the stones coming to life once a year at Hunter's Moon (the first moon after the full moon nearest to the autumn equinox - which is about 23 September).

A discrepancy will be noticed in the number of stones. This is not surprising as according to superstition no two counts of standing stones are ever the same. The optimum figure here seems to be sixteen or seventeen.

Dartmoor is littered with prehistoric remains - stone avenues, stone tombs ('cists'), single standing stones ('menhirs') and circles. The full story behind their purpose will probably never be known but the smaller circles, such as this one, usually encircle burial mounds.

There is a tradition that it is dangerous to tamper with any of the stones and William Crossing, the Dartmoor historian, records that when a cist (191/734755) at Widecombe was opened by a former parson his house was destroyed by an explosion the following night.

Scorhill stone circle (191/655874) on Gidleigh Common, one of the larger ones, has the reputation of scaring horses and riders have to make a detour.

And why the name? Folklore has it that the maidens were turned to stone for dancing on the sabbath. Perhaps there is a confusion here between the 'sabbath' and witchcraft 'sabbats' or ritual festivals (from the old French 's'*esbattre*' meaning 'to frolic'). Nine has a tradition as a 'magical number' and because of the sun and moon the circle would have been an important feature of bygone nature worship and witchcraft.

Maybe it is not really the stones that dance on Belstone Common after all.

Crazywell Pool

(202/582705)

This lonely expanse of water, over an acre in area, lies on the high moor between Sheepstor and Princetown.

It is said that at various times in the past a voice has been heard calling loudly from the water with the name of the next person in the parish to die. For this reason people who worked on the moors would walk several miles out of their way rather than pass anywhere near it.

Another version of the superstition maintains that an image of the next person to die will appear in the pool on midsummer's eve.

Recently two local youths were challenged to spend midsummer's eve at Crazywell. As they rode home later that night the motor bike they were on failed to negotiate a bend on Roborough Down and both were killed.

What had they seen in the pool? Their own reflections?

Legend also has it that the River Dart claims lives, one per year, and can be heard calling for its victim beforehand. Hence the old rhyme:

> River of Dart, O river of Dart,
> Every year thou claimest a heart.

Supernatural phenomena are often associated with water and there is a theory that the special electrical field of water acts as a kind of tape recorder of strong emotions. Underground water was possibly of the greatest importance to prehistoric people in the siting of their monuments.

Dartmoor has innumerable rivers and streams, much boggy terrain that is sometimes watery, eight reservoirs and several flooded mines, but no natural lakes or pools. Although Crazywell Pool is the result of tin working it is distinguished from other artificial waters on the moor by the hidden spring that feeds it.

▰ Jay's Grave, Childe's Tomb ▰ and Fitz's Wells

(191/732798, 202/618703, 191/592939 and 191/577758)

The first two of these well-known features illustrate the grimmer side of Dartmoor's past, prettified by folklore.

The pitiful story of Kitty or Mary Jay takes place in the eighteenth century. A servant girl and orphan, abandoned by her lover and carrying his child, she hanged herself.

She was buried near Manaton where three parish boundaries meet as none would claim responsibility for her, at a crossroads so that her spirit would not be able to find its way back to its former haunts and bother anyone. (One arm of the crossroads is now a footpath.)

In about 1860 the spot was disturbed by a road mender and the bones of a young woman found. The man reburied these in a coffin and restored the grave. Since then the grave is always decorated with a pot of flowers, although no one admits to putting it there.

In a local television programme in 1978 a young woman under hypnosis appeared to recall a previous life as Kitty Jay and described in harrowing detail the last few weeks of the orphan's life.

Childe was a hunter caught in a blizzard at nightfall on the desolate and deadly Foxtor Mires (202/610700). In desperation he slaughtered his horse and huddled inside the still-warm carcass for protection. To no avail however for his body was later found frozen to death at the spot where his monument now stands.

Sadly nothing of his 'tomb' - rectangular granite blocks topped with a rough granite cross - is original as the site was restored at the end of last century. Beneath it however is a chamber which may be a prehistoric tomb.

It is thought that the protagonist was either a fourteenth-century Amyas Childe or the eleventh-century son of a Saxon earl of Devon, 'Childe' deriving from 'cild', a Saxon title of honour.

The body was found by monks and there is a story that before the Second World War two girls visiting the area and apparently knowing nothing of its history saw a party of monks with a bier approaching their car. They switched off their engine and waited for the procession to pass but as it came level with them it vanished.

A cross with a different purpose is that marking Fitz's Well near Okehampton. This is supposed to be a holy well and anyone who drinks from it on Easter Sunday will be married within a year or have good luck for a year. Unfortunately the well is now covered.

John Fitz, the grandfather of Lady Howard whose ghost rides out nightly from Fitzford House, put up the cross in the sixteenth century.

There are stone crosses all over the moor, the majority thought to be medieval waymarks. Some of these ancient tracks such as the Abbot's Way (from Buckfast Abbey in the east to Buckland Abbey in the west) and the Lich Way (from Bellever to Lydford) still exist and can be found on maps.

There is another Fitz's Well near Princetown, sometimes called Fice's Well. Here John Fitz put a canopy over a spring, and on it the initials I[J]F and the date, 1568, can still just be seen.

According to legend Fitz and his wife were 'pixy-led' while out on the moor but restored by drinking from the wells. He erected the memorials in gratitude.

Lydford

I oft have heard of Lydford Law
How in the morn they hang and draw
And sit in judgement after.

Twelfth-century Lydford Castle used to be a prison for offenders against Dartmoor's strict hunting and tin-working laws. Judge Jeffreys, notorious for his harshness, is said to haunt it in the shape of a black boar.

People from far into the moor had to bring their dead to Lydford Church for burial, travelling along the Lich Way ('lich' meaning a body, alive or dead). Small wonder that phantom funeral processions are sometimes seen making their way along the ancient track.

In the sixteenth century the caves of the steep and rocky gorge below the castle sheltered a degenerate tribe of thieves called the Gubbins who terrorized the area. Charles Kingsley, who was born at Holne, wrote about them in *Westward Ho!*

At one end of the gorge is a dark pool of swirling water called the Devil's Cauldron and at another pool called Kit's Steps the ghost of an old lady in a red headscarf has been seen.

In spite of its sombre past Lydford today attracts many visitors.

Spinsters' Rock

(191/700908)

This neolithic burial chamber is the only example of its kind in Devon and probably the oldest prehistoric monument on the moor.

According to legend its three seven-foot-high granite rocks with their sixteen-ton stone 'lid' were put up by a band of stalwart lady spinners (not necessarily unmarried) one morning before breakfast.

Although the structure did collapse in 1862 and has been re-erected, it is difficult to see any meaning in the legend. One possibility is that the 'spinners' are related to Belstone's 'maidens' (see page 20) and the name is a veiled reference to witchcraft.

There is a tradition on the moor that standing stones will fall on to faithless wives and flatten them. Perhaps there is another connection here!

'Ley' hunters say that Spinsters' Rock stands on one of these straight energy lines through natural features and ancient monuments. It is also claimed that it was built to mark a meeting place of underground springs, an especially sacred place to prehistoric people.

Bowerman's Nose

(191/742804)

On Hayne Down near Manaton, a short walk from the road, rises an unmistakable tor with the profile of a bulbous-nosed man in a peaked cap.

At one time people believed that the tors were massive religious sculptures like the stone figures on Easter Island, put up by the Celtic priesthood, the Druids. On many of the tors are loose basin-shaped rocks which the Druids were supposed to have made for catching the blood of their sacrifices. The lines and cracks in the tors were a form of writing.

Scientists however say that the tors are natural granite outcrops and that all their features can be explained by the action of weather.

Usually in Dartmoor's legends the witches are worsted and the huntsmen are all powerful. Thankfully the roles are reversed here.

Bowerman was a 'bowman' who disturbed a coven of witches. In revenge they turned him and his hounds to stone. The hounds can be seen at nearby Hound Tor (191/742790) and sometimes on dark nights you can still hear them baying.

Alternatively, the name comes from the Celtic *vawr-maen*, 'great stone'.

The Dewerstone

(SX538639)

In the far south-western corner of the moor above the meeting place of the Rivers Plym and Meavy is an awesome crag said to be the home of Dewer, Dartmoor's phantom huntsman. With his fearsome Wisht Hounds (see pages 8-9) he pursues lone travellers over the sheer rock face to their death below. The foot of the rock is haunted by a black dog.

Cloven hoofed and horned, Dewer is a figure with counterparts in many cultures. To Christians he is the devil and hunts the souls of unbaptized babies.

A farmer, coming home late at night somewhat the worse for wear, met up with the demon huntsman. Not realizing who he was he asked him what he had caught that day.

Laughing, the huntsman handed over his catch telling the farmer to keep it.

The farmer hurried off, thinking with pleasure of the good supper he was going to have that night.

When he got home he unwrapped the bundle and found inside it not some tasty small animal or bird but instead the dead body of his own child.

Enough to turn anyone back to the straight and narrow.

══ *Sayings and Superstitions* ══

To cure shingles make a wreath of rushes, put it over the affected area of skin and then hang it up inside a chimney. Do this three times.

To get rid of chilblains you should wish them on to someone just dead.

A collar of woven ash twigs or a hazel wand put round the neck of an animal bitten by an adder will cure it.

Snake skin will repel thorns so if you have a thorn on one side of your finger put some snake skin on the other side.

Don't keep kittens born in May because when adult they will bring in snakes.

Where an adder lies hidden, a dragonfly hovers above.

Drawing a witch's blood, even that from a pin prick, will break any spell cast by that witch.

The first direct glance from a black witch contains the malevolent influence so you must divert this by wearing bright buttonholes or hanging up things like coloured glass balls, bunches of flowers or branches with lots of berries.

Witches must not discuss their power or it will leave them. Nor must they accept money, for the same reason.

Beware of the wych elm - it is used in witchcraft.

Dill, vervain, mountain ash, St John's wort, trefoil, elder, garlic, verbena, bracken and pennywort all guard against evil influences.

Setting fire to growing ferns produces rain.

If a circle is drawn round a hen and the bird is then carried round it with its beak to the circumference it will stay in the circle.

Will o' the wisp is the spirit of an animal that has sunk into the bog and died.

Lambs must not be tailed when the moon is waning as the bleeding will not stop until the moon has 'turned'.

Don't pick stitchwort or you run the risk of being 'pixy-led'.

The ringing of church bells is a good way to deter pixies.

He who in July the cuckoo's voice doth hear
Will die before he comes another year.

To hear the first cry of the cuckoo on your right is lucky; on your left unlucky.

Gelding should be carried out on Good Friday and children weaned, but no clothes washing should be done or one of the family will be 'washed clean' (die) before the year is out.

She who cuts dough with a knife
Will ne'er be happy, maid, widow or wife.

Calendar

TWELFTH NIGHT - (5/6 January)
Wassailing in orchards - singing, drinking cider and making noise to scare away
evil spirits and ensure plenty of apples later in the year

CANDLEMAS - (2 February)
First of four main witches' sabbats (and Church festival)

LADY DAY - (25 March)
Fairs for hiring workers

COLLOP MONDAY - (Monday before Lent)
Collops (slices of meat), eggs and pancakes eaten

LENSHARD DAY - (Tuesday before Lent)
Children called at houses for pancake ingredients and threw broken crockery (Lent 'shards') in the doorway of anyone who didn't contribute

> *Pan kakes an' fritters*
> *Us be come for,*
> *If you don't give us some,*
> *Us'll bang down the door*

EASTER
Fitz's Well, Okehampton, visited
Sunrise service on Yes Tor (191/580902)

BELLEVER DAY - (soon after Easter)
Beginning of a week's hare hunting on Bellever Tor (191/644764)

TAIL-PIPE DAY - (1 April)
Tomfoolery such as attaching notices to other people's backs

MAY DAY/BELTANE - (1 May)
Beacons lit on hills
Second of four main witches' sabbats
Dancing tree celebrations at Moretonhampstead - a platform was put in a sacred tree and people danced on it. Similar celebrations at many sacred trees.
*Maypole dancing

STINGING-NETTLE DAY - (3 May)
Children beat each other with nettles

BEATING THE BOUNDS - (1st Monday after 3 May at Bovey Tracey)
Villagers walked round parish boundaries beating the boundary stones with sticks.
Conducted in many other parishes at different times.

OAK-APPLE DAY/GARLAND DAY - (29 May)
People decorated themselves and their houses with oak apples and oak leaves
General festivities

WHITSUN - (7th week after Easter)
Fairs and games, especially at Widecombe

TRINITY - (8th week after Easter)
Fairs and games
Gooseberry pasties and cream traditional fare at Drewsteignton
*Drinking, dancing and skittles at Meavy Oak

MIDSUMMER'S DAY - (24 June)
Fire and water ceremonies and a time for seeing into the future
Sheep sacrifice at Buckland
Ram roasting at Holne (also possibly on 5/6 July)
Rolling of a burning wheel at Buckfastleigh

BEATING THE BOUNDS - (17 July)
At Buckfastleigh

LAMMAS - (1 August)
Third of four main witches' sabbats
Also called Feast of the First Fruits

*ASHBURTON ST LAWRENCE FAIR - (10 August)
Dating from at least fourteenth century with bull baiting, ale tasting, bread weighing and pig droving

BEATING THE BOUNDS - (last week in August)
At Gidleigh

*MORETONHAMPSTEAD FAIR - (last week in August)

*WIDECOMBE FAIR - (2nd Tuesday in September)

> *Tom Pearse, Tom Pearse, lend me your grey mare,*
> *All along, down along, out along, leigh,*
> *For I want to go to Widecombe Fair,*
> *All along, down along, out along, leigh.*

With Bill Brewer, Jan Stewer, Peter Davey, Peter Gurney,
Daniel Whiddon, Harry Hawk, Old Uncle Tom Cobley and all,
Old Uncle Tom Cobley and all

World famous because of the traditional song and a very popular event

MICHAELMAS - (29 September)
'Giglet' fairs for hiring workers

*TAVISTOCK GOOSE (OR GOOSEY) FAIR
(Until last century on Michaelmas Day, 29 September, now 2nd Wednesday in October)

At least eight hundred years old. Roast goose was traditional Michaelmas fare. Thousands of geese would be driven to Tavistock and then on to London, with shoemakers en route to make small soft leather shoes for any geese that became lame. Today it draws people instead. Nineteenth-century roundabout, funfair and livestock auctions.

HARVEST
'Crying the neck' - ceremonial gathering in of last sheaf of corn

HALLOWE'EN - (31 October)
Eve of pagan new year
Fourth main witches' sabbat

ST ANDREW'S DAY - (4th Thursday in November)
Feasting and sports at Moretonhampstead

CHRISTMAS - (25 December)
'Ashen faggots' (ash twigs and branches bound together) were burnt in homes
Mumming plays at Ashburton and Bovey Tracey

* These events still take place in one form or another. There are many fairs and festivals at villages and towns throughout the moor from March to November. For up-to-date information see the free annual newsheet *The Dartmoor Visitor*, available from local public libraries, or contact the Dartmoor National Park Headquarters, Haytor Road, Bovey Tracey, Devon TQ13 9QJ, telephone 0626 832093.

Books

Copley, Len, and Gant,Tom *Dartmoor Legends Retold* (Baron Jay nd)
- *More Dartmoor Legends and Customs* (Baron Jay nd)

Coxhead, J R W *Legends of Devon* (Western Press 1954)
- *Old Devon Customs* (Raleigh Press 1957)
- *Devon Traditions and Fairy Tales* (Raleigh Press 1959)
- *The Devil in Devon* (West Country Handbooks 1967)
- *Ghosts in Devon* (Town and Country Press 1972)

Devon Folklife Register *Folk Festivals and Traditions of Devon* (Exeter City Museums Service 1980)

Farquharson-Coe, A *Devon Witchcraft* (James Pike 1975)

Grinsell, Leslie V *Folklore of Prehistoric Sites in Britain* (David & Charles 1976)

Hippisley Coxe, Antony D *Haunted Britain* (Hutchinson 1973)

Leger-Gordon, Ruth St *The Witchcraft and Folklore of Dartmoor* (Robert Hale 1965)

Pegg, John *After Dark on Dartmoor* (John Pegg 1984)
- *The Face of Dartmoor* (John Pegg 1988)

Starkey, F H *Dartmoor Crosses and Some Ancient Tracks* (F H Starkey 1983)
- *Odds and Ends from Dartmoor* (F H Starkey 1984)

Weir, John (ed) *Dartmoor National Park* (Webb & Bower/Michael Joseph 1987) (Countryside Commission official guide)

Whitlock, Ralph *The Folklore of Devon* (Batsford 1977)

Wilson, Colin (intro by) *Westcountry Mysteries* (Bossiney Books 1985)

Wreford, Hilary, and Williams, Michael *Mysteries in the Devon Landscape* (Bossiney Books 1985)

A
Glimpse of
DARTMOOR
TORS

John Risdon

Peninsula
Press

Dedicated to my sister, Jill.
'Your spirit is as free as the wind
and the open sky.'

Published by Peninsula Press Ltd
P.O. Box 31
Newton Abbot
Devon TQ12 5XH

Tel: 0803 875875

Printed in England by D.D.S. Colour Printers, Weston-Super-Mare.

ISBN 1 872640 07 9

The map of Dartmoor on pages 16-17 is reproduced with the kind
permission of the Dartmoor National Park Authority.

Photographs by the author.

A GLIMPSE OF DARTMOOR
· TORS ·

Contents

Introduction 5

How tors came into being 7

Tors along the Ashburton/Two Bridges road 9

Tors along the Two Bridges/Moretonhampstead road 13

Tors along the Two Bridges/Yelverton road 15

Map of Dartmoor and Glossary 16

Tors along the Tavistock/Two Bridges road 21

Tors along the Bovey Tracey/Widecombe Road 25

Tors along the Tavistock /Okehampton Road 29

Bel Tor

Introduction

Dartmoor National Park consists of an area some 365 sq.miles in extent, 250 sq.miles being open moorland, sprinkled with isolated village and farming communities on the lower slopes and in sheltered valleys. The higher and wilder area of moorland is divided in two by a belt of lowland identified by, and associated with, the route of the main Tavistock/Ashburton road. These two areas are respectively known as the North and South Moors.

On driving up onto, and across the moors, one recurring natural feature that comes into view, with a tendency to catch the eye, is the Dartmoor tor, a mound of granite rock sitting starkly on the skyline or hillside. Tors are as variable in appearance as they are numerous. From ruined medieval castle to cartoon character, from dramatic to comical, the shapes often look man-made, and yet all are the result of natural forces shaping the granite rock over millions of years. The majority of tors are situated around the edges of the two 'high moor' areas and are (weather permitting) visible from many vantage points along the roads and lanes of Dartmoor. A number are also easily accessible from the road for closer inspection.

On the following pages, your attention will be drawn to the various tors to be seen as you drive across the moors. Some points of interest, geographical, historical and legendary, are explained, and it is hoped that this will encourage a brief expedition, weather permitting, to explore one of these moorland crags and let your senses experience the delights of Dartmoor at first hand. Heights and map references (Ordnance Survey maps, Landranger 191 and 202) are included for each tor.

For practical purposes this book describes tors visible whilst driving, riding or walking along any one of six major routes across the moor. To assist the motorist in stopping safely so that the view can be admired, or the car left whilst a walk is undertaken, the National Park has provided regular 'off the road ' parking areas. Stopping on the road itself, or pulling off onto the grass verge should not be contemplated.

The Author

Born and bred in Devon, and with a career spanning the worlds of education and book-selling, John Risdon has, over 40 years, gained an intimate knowledge of an area which, in his own words, has become part of his very being, developed through the soles of his feet, and the senses of sight, sound and feeling, together with the learned words of those like-minded Dartmoor folk that he has been lucky enough to spend time with.

◆

Sharp Tor

══How Tors Came Into Being══

Whilst viewing or scrambling over one of these impressive tors the question must arise in one's mind - 'How did they get there?'

Some 300 million years ago, the granite of which Dartmoor consists, was injected as a semi-liquid material into a huge subterranean area, many thousands of feet beneath the Earth's surface. Here it gradually cooled and solidified into solid rock. As the cooling was in progress the thousands of feet of rock above the granite were gradually eroded away: a process which took over 200 million years. Finally the granite itself became exposed.

As this process was taking place, relieved of the incredible weight of overlying rock, the granite expanded and a complex system of horizontal and vertical cracks (joints) came into being. These joints allowed ground water to seep into the rock, where due to acidity, it gradually ate away at the rock itself, breaking it up into small particles. Some areas of rock were more heavily jointed than others and were broken up more substantially.

Between 600,000 and 10,000 years ago the Earth experienced a series of Ice Ages. The ice sheets did not cover what is now Dartmoor but the climate here was similar to Northern Canada today; long periods of extreme cold with intermittent thaws causing huge quantities of melt water to pour down over this granite area. With the granite now also exposed to the surface, water freezing and expanding in the joints, helped to continue the process of breaking up the granite. Melt water then assisted in washing away the broken material.

Over hundreds of thousands of years the original granite surface has been eroded away, leaving the less jointed, more resistant areas fighting a rearguard action against the forces of nature. These are the tors of Dartmoor, which are themselves being gradually eaten away.

At the base of every tor, and hidden in every joint, can be found the course grains of granite that have 'recently' broken away from their parent rock. Scattered on the slopes beneath many tors are the remains of what were once even more immense structures. These boulders or 'clitter', as they are known, were broken off by the intense cold during the ice ages and then skidded downhill over the 'ice-rink' surface to their present resting place.

The Dartmoor landscape, crowned with its rugged tors, is a dramatic one, as was its formation.

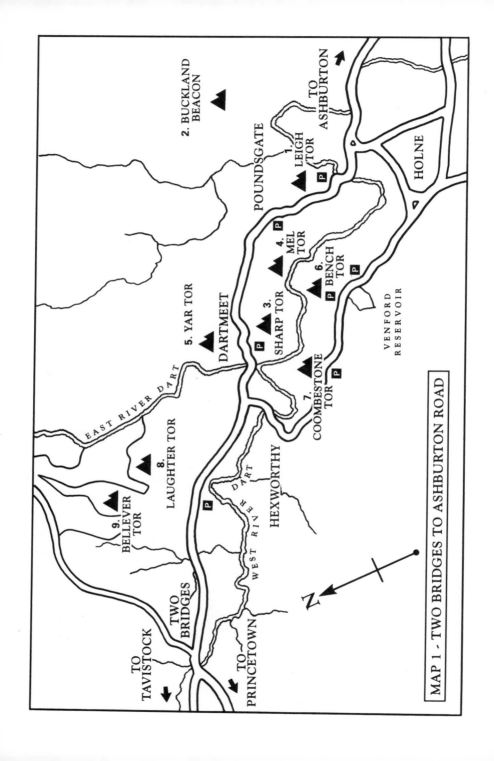

MAP 1 - TWO BRIDGES TO ASHBURTON ROAD

═══*Tors along the Ashburton/*═══ *Two Bridges Road - map 1*

Climbing up onto the moors from New Bridge (1) LEIGH TOR 150m (712715) is prominent on the side of the hill, being the first tor to be seen close at hand, when driving up from Ashburton. Situated to the north of the road overlooking the River Dart at Spitchwick this fine example illustrates the fact that tors are not necessarily on the summits of hills. This tor is much used for novice climbing instruction, something not to be undertaken unless under professional guidance.

Visible from the stretch of road above Leigh Tor, in a north-easterly direction, is the isolated mound of (2) BUCKLAND BEACON 380m (735732). Standing out on the skyline this particular beacon is in fact a tor, its strategic position making it an ideal spot for signalling in times past.

On the south-west facing slope of this tor can be found 'The Ten Commandments', cut into two slabs of granite in 1928 on the instructions of William Whitley, the lord of the manor at that time. The view from the beacon is one of the most breathtaking there is, and the walk from the Ashburton to Widecombe road cattlegrid at 738738 is by no means arduous, with all the climbing having been done by the car!

Having climbed up steeply from the river at Dartmeet or New Bridge, the road runs relatively level with the Dart valley to the south. Within a quarter mile of the road, on the south side, stands mighty (3) SHARP TOR 380m (687730). This tor caps a mighty hill, with only the top 50 metres visible from the road. From across the river at (6) BENCH TOR, or along the Hexworthy/Holne road, Sharp Tor can be seen in full perspective, as the conical capping on the summit of the Dart valley side, with the river murmuring 180 metres below.

Sharp Tor acts as an apt memorial to the spirits of the moor and river, and specifically 'Jan Coo', a farmer's boy who perished in the river below. It is said he was enticed by the river pixies, much warned of by family and friends, never to be seen again.

> *River of Dart, O river of Dart,*
> *Every year thou claimest a heart.*

A neighbouring tor to Sharp, although not visible from the road, is well worth a visit. This is (4) MEL TOR 346m (695726), situated downstream with a dominating position overlooking the Dart Gorge, as this section of the valley is known. Mel Tor is situated on a natural shelf, above the gorge, along which a carriage drive was constructed by a Dr Blackall, Lord of Spitchwick Manor, during the late 19th century. Today, this drive, now a rough track, makes for ideal access on foot, allowing superb views of the gorge, the river, and tors positioned as natural ramparts, along the rim. Access to the drive is either from its junction with the main road at 707716, where it levels off after its climb up from New Bridge, just before the Poundsgate sign, or, the parking area to the south of the road immediately the summit has been gained at 695732 (During the summer one ice-cream van in position).

A short detour has to be made from the drive to Mel Tor, but your efforts will be well rewarded with both the view and also some fine examples of rock basins. In bygone days Mel Tor was the site for despatching blazing cartwheels down the side of the gorge on Midsummer's Day. Very much a common happening in the past, throughout Devon, the last such event was recorded here in the 1950's.

Returning to the road from Sharp Tor and equidistant to the north west, stands (5) YAR TOR 416m (678740). More visible when climbing up the road from Dartmeet, this tor, situated on the summit of the hill, gives an excellent view of the valley below and the moorland beyond. Very close to Yar Tor can be found examples of a cairn, a cist, and a stone row; three remains of life from the Bronze Age.

Across the Dart Gorge from Mel Tor, can be seen (6) BENCH (or Benjy) TOR 312m (692717). Standing precipitously on the lip of the gorge, it is itself dramatic (including one of its rock stacks aptly named 'Eagle Rock') but also offers the most dramatic view of the gorge. The easiest access to this tor is from the car park above Venford Reservoir, this being situated on the Hexworthy/Holne loop road (see map). A half-mile walk from the car park, over relatively level moorland, brings you to what seems a rather unexciting, low summit - and there, suddenly, 170 metres below, tumbles the mighty Dart.

A second tor accessible from this loop road, but nearer to Hexworthy, is (7) COOMBESTONE TOR 356m (671718). Complete with its own car park, this tor is a mere 50 metres from the road with a view of Dartmeet to the north. Its easy access gives the car user an excellent opportunity to view the natural phenomenon of a rock basin without much effort. Walk past the tor and downhill a few metres and the man-made phenomenon of a Dartmoor leat may also be viewed. This particular waterway was cut to take water from the nearby O'brook stream to provide for the needs of Holne village and the more distant Buckfastleigh woollen mills.

Returning to the main Ashburton/Two Bridges road, west of Dartmeet, two tors to the north of the road are certainly worthy of attention. From a distance both are best viewed from the car park at 639748, situated to the north of the road, between two relatively conspicuous bridges. The right-hand of the two, (8) LAUGHTER TOR 420m (653756) situated one mile from the road, is the less conspicuous of the two but is surrounded by many remains of bygone days including a bronze age menhir (standing stone) and a pound (enclosure) of ambiguous age.

The name of this tor has nothing to do with mirth, but shows how local dialect and the passage of time can change names nearly beyond recognition. The name of this particular tor a century ago was LOUGH TOR, lough being a term used in local agriculture.

To the north west of Laughter and one mile distant, stands the more prominent (9) BELLEVER TOR 443m (644764). Conspicuous in its cloak of 20th century plantation conifers, Bellever Tor has been a focal point of both life and death on the moor for generations past. A multitude of Bronze Age burial sites are to be found within close proximity to the tor, and into this century the tor has been the assembly point for the local hunt.

For easier access to these two tors, Laughter can best be reached by footpath from nearby Dunnabridge Pound (644747), and Bellever from Postbridge (647788), with a walk up through Bellever Forest. A direct approach from the car park at 639748 is not advised, especially in wet conditions.

Should you be travelling in the Two Bridges direction or are in the car park last mentioned, at 639748, weather permitting, you will notice the distant, westerly skyline with its tors silhouetted against the sky, as ships steaming in line-a-head. Although visible from this road, reference to them is made in the Two Bridges/Moretonhampstead section.

Coombestone Tor

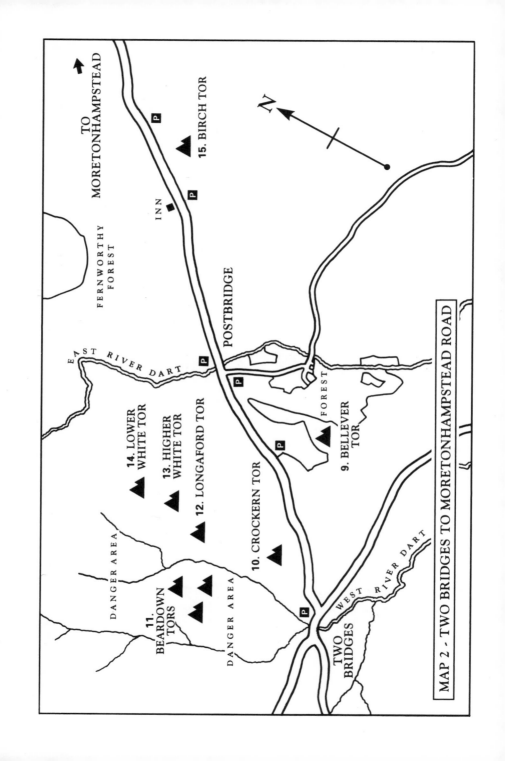

MAP 2 - TWO BRIDGES TO MORETONHAMPSTEAD ROAD

▬*Tors along the Two Bridges/* ▬ *Moretonhampstead Road - map 2*

The majority of tors visible from this route lie to the north of the road and are concentrated towards the Two Bridges area.

On leaving Two Bridges the first tor, being very close to the road on the left, comes into sight as soon as the first rise is surmounted. One's first observation might in fact overlook the tor entirely as it is very fragmented and rather unimpressive from the road. However (10) CROCKERN TOR 400m (616758), situated on the hillside, could be said to be the most historically important tor on Dartmoor, certainly in a social context. It was here that the early tin miners held their stannary court, or parliament, and made their laws; laws which directed and controlled, not only the tinner's lives, but also the lives of all the inhabitants of Dartmoor during the Middle Ages, from the early 14th century until the mid 18th century.

The reason Crockern Tor was chosen for this purpose was its central position on the moor, being roughly equidistant from the stannary towns of Ashburton, Chagford and Tavistock, each with their own area of moorland and tinners. The tor also presented a natural shape likened to an amphitheatre, allowing the hundred or so members of the court to sit in such a way that they could hear one another reasonably well, even in poor weather.

Closely associated with this stannary court was Lydford Castle where breakers of the tinners' laws could find themseves imprisoned. Should you wish to inspect this fascinating tor more closely, please note that parking off the road, adjacent to the tor, is very limited. It would be preferable to use the car park provided for your use at Two Bridges, with a short walk up across the moor to the tor.

Set back from the road, on ridges either side of the West Dart, are a series of more visible tor structures, although not within such easy reach of the road. These four tors are described on page 9 , as seen from the Ashburton/Two Bridges road. The most westerly, and visible from around Crockern Tor, is (or are), (11)the BEARDOWN TORS group 511m (605775), being in fact four separate stacks, three large, one smaller.

The area around Beardown has for some time been the home of a herd of highland cattle, a long way from their native homeland but well suited to this local environment of granite and peat.

Moving east, and clearly visible from the road as you drive away from Two Bridges, is the large conical shape of (12) LONGAFORD TOR 507m (616779) on the skyline.

To its right is first, (13) HIGHER WHITE TOR 527m (620786), followed by (14) LOWER WHITE TOR 507m (619793). These tors of the West Dart act as sentinels to the North Moor. To the south-east they look down over the central basin of Dartmoor; once past them, heading north-west, the intruder finds the open vastness of the high moor, with its plateau of peat hags and an uninterrupted skyline, open to all weathers and providing little shelter for the unprepared walker.

On the opposite side of the road, to the east, stands (9) BELLEVER TOR 443m. Cloaked within its own conifer plantation, this centre of Bronze Age life and death, is easily identified as it stands in its own glorious isolation, dominating the woodland below. *For further details see entry under Ashburton/Two Bridges Road.*

The last tor to be noted on this route lies to the east of the road, some two miles north-east of Postbridge. This is (15) BIRCH TOR 487m (687817). Situated in what was an intensively mined area, the tor is best viewed from the car park by the Warren House Inn, the only building on this stretch of the road. On the hillside beneath the tor notice the walled enclosures built by the mining fraternity for rabbiting and vegetable growing, in the shape of playing card symbols! Called 'Jan Reynold's Cards', legend has it that the said gentleman was carried off by the devil for playing cards in Widecombe Church. On passing over this spot he dropped the cards which, on hitting the ground, immediately turned to stone.

Thought to be the Judge's Chair from the Tinners' Court at Crochern Tor, now to be found at Huccaby Pond

═Tors along the Two Bridges/═ Yelverton Road - map 3

On approaching Princetown, be it from Two Bridges or Yelverton, a tor, although barely visible from the road, is the best marked on Dartmoor. This is (16) NORTH HESSARY TOR 517m (578743), situated at the base of a T.V. transmission mast of that name. The tor itself, is small in size, with the majority of its original mass now scattered on the surrounding slopes as clitter, deposited during the ice ages. Accessible by footpath from the Princetown Tourist Information Centre, this tor, on the crown of one of the higher hills in this area, provides excellent views, on mist free days, of West Devon, and Cornwall in the far distance.

On the western hill slopes below the summit, visible from certain roadside vantage points, but not from North Hessary Tor, can be found the remains of two very interesting and unusual tors (17) FOGGINTOR 400m (567736) and (18) SWELL TOR 400m (560733). Both tors, providing good quality granite, have been largely removed by quarrying activity which took place up to the early part of this century. Granite from here was used to construct the prison at Princetown, and of even greater note, the stone for Nelson's Column was cut and dressed in this very place before being transported to Trafalgar Square.

Many examples of the quarrymens' and stonemasons' skills still remain at these quarries for the visitor to see. A walk along the track from its junction with the Tavistock/Princetown road at (567750 by the pumphouse) to Foggintor will provide a worthwhile experience of a bygone era.

Returning to the Two Bridges/Yelverton road, south-west of Princetown and north of the road, (19) LEEDEN TOR 380m (564718) can be seen peaking out from its position on the shoulder of the hill which tends to obscure it from the road. A relatively large tor, it contains a number of rock basins and is within easy reach of the two car parks shown on the map.

Across the road from Leeden, but further away from the car parks, is (20) BLACK TOR 360m (574718). Although smaller in size, this tor contains excellent examples of both a logan stone and rock basin. Also within easy reach are a stone row and cairn. Much of interest to search for in one short excursion.

Across the valley from Black Tor, to the north-west, is (21) HART TOR 390m (582720), named after the white hart deer which were once found around

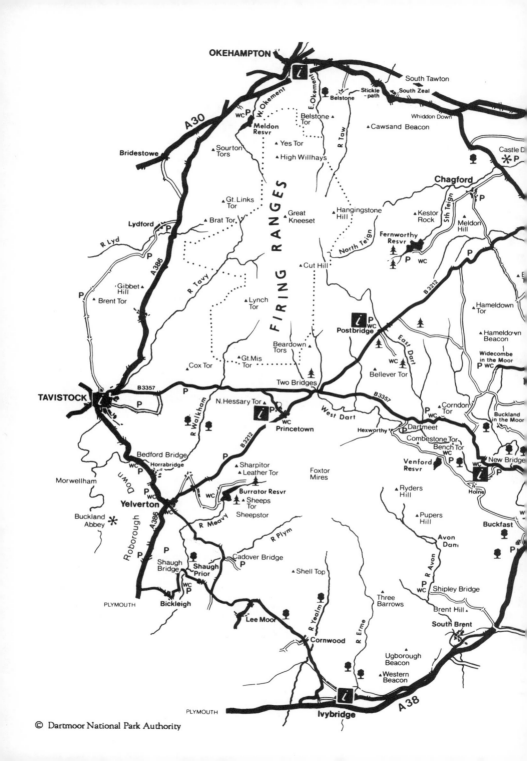

DARTMOOR

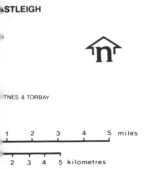

EXETER

EXETER

NEWTON ABBOT

NEWTON ABBOT

A30

R Telgn

Dunsford
Steps Bridge
P WC
i

Bridford
▲ Blackingstone Rock

etonhampstead

Christow

Kennick
Trenchford
& Tottiford
Resvrs
P

Hennock

Lustleigh
Becky Falls

HQ

Bovey Tracey

WC P   Ilsington

A38

ASHBURTON

STLEIGH

TNES & TORBAY

```
1   2   3   4   5  miles
|___|___|___|___|___|

2   3   4   5  kilometres
|___|___|___|___|
```

KEY

i Dartmoor National Park Information Centre

P Parking   **WC** Toilets

GLOSSARY

CAIRNE or BARROW
A marker of granite boulders, variable in size. Built over a cist to mark the site, or possibly to help in protecting the grave from robbers, wild animal or human in type.

CIST or KISTVANE
A Bronze Age burial chamber made of granite slabs. Quite small in size and usually buried, or partially buried, in the peat, they held either a curled up body or cremated ashes in an urn.

LOGAN STONE
A granite boulder which can be rocked on its base. Caused by the removal of fragmented granite material, leaving only one pivot point.

MENHIR - Standing stone

POUND - Enclosure for animals

ROCK BASIN
The natural carving of a basin shape within the granite, etched out over thousands of years. Caused by the erosive action of granite particles in a water-filled pool, as water and particles are moved by the power of the wind in a circular motion.

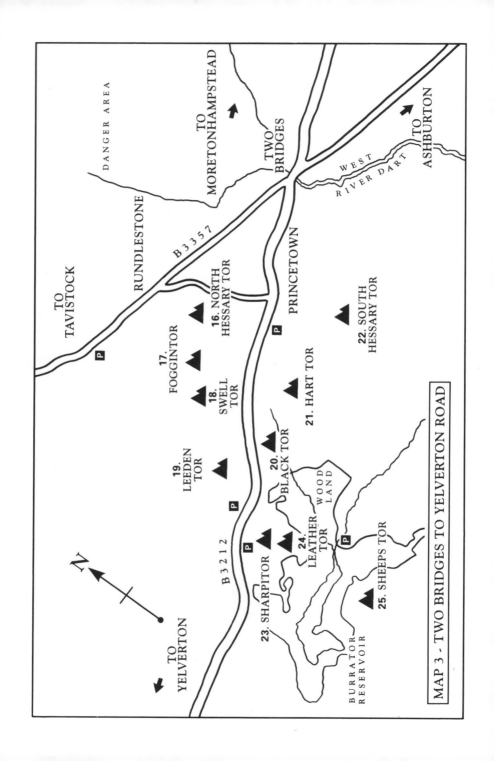

MAP 3 - TWO BRIDGES TO YELVERTON ROAD

this area. On the skyline beyond, notice the small blip that is (22) SOUTH HESSARY TOR 450m (597724), less big sister's T.V. mast.

One fact that does unit these two tors as well as their name, is that they are both boundary marks laid down in the year 1240 by twelve knights to identify the 'Forest of Dartmoor' as an exclusive hunting ground for the King's use. This area remains as 'The Forest of Dartmoor' today being officially the property of HRH The Prince of Wales.

Remaining on this side of the road, moving south-west, most dramatically seen on route towards Yelverton, are the two separate masses of (23) SHARPITOR 410m (560705), nearest the road, and (24) LEATHER TOR 360m (563700). Peak Hill, on which they both sit, rises up steeply from Burrator Reservoir, to the south. Both offer superb views over Burrator and the surrounding countryside, from Sharpitor on the crown of the hill, and from Leather Tor, situated on a steep ridge with an impressive vertical height of 70 metres from top to bottom.

Two well situated car parks on either side of the road as it skirts the north slope of Peek Hill, provide ideal parking should you wish to explore these two great tors on the very edge of the moor.

To the south-east, across the woodland enclosed reservoir, stands the heavily fragmented but conspicuous (25) SHEEPS TOR 369m (566683) with its petite hamlet of like name, tucked in cosily at its southern foot.

Near the summit can be found a small cave in the clitter, named 'The Pixie's House'. Legend has it that during the Civil War, refugees from the Parliamentarian forces were hidden here by the local villagers.

The moorland around this tor is also well-known for its rabbit warrens. Encouraged and looked after by miners and local farmers, these were man-made enclosures created for the raising of rabbits. This was the main source of meat for the locals and also provided a very popular product for sale in the nearby Plymouth markets.

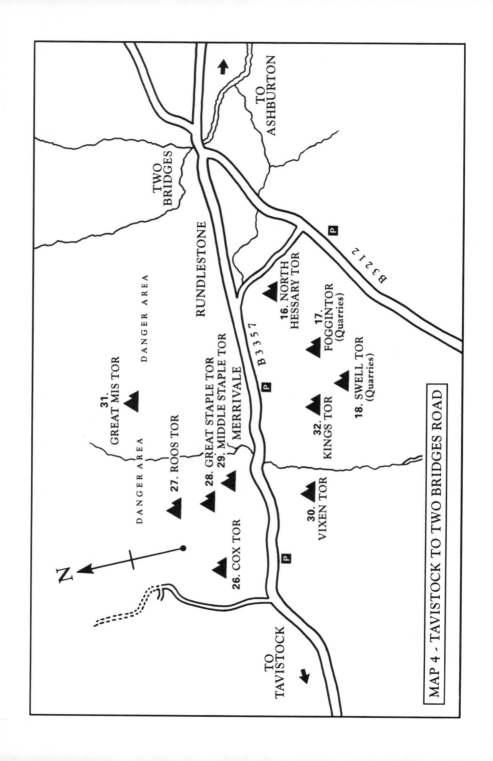

MAP 4 - TAVISTOCK TO TWO BRIDGES ROAD

▰▰▰ *Tors along the Tavistock/* ▰▰▰
Two Bridges Road - map 4

On your journeys along the roads of Dartmoor there are a number of stopping places that can offer you the immediate feeling of total openess and space. One such place is the car park at the summit of the climb out of Tavistock (531752), just over the cattle grid. From here the majority of tors visible from this road can be seen in one sweep through 180 degrees.

To the north of the car park, hanging on the very edge of Dartmoor, rises (26) COX (COCKS) TOR 442m (531762). Rising up on a long, grassy, concave slope, this natural outlook over West Devon, Plymouth, the Sound, and much of Cornwall, can add a further 80 metres of height to your view.

Pivoting to the right, three tors make a natural grouping along one ridge. Most distant is (27) ROOS TOR 454m (543767). Providing examples of both logan stone and rock basin, this tor marks the last rock outcrop, if progressing north, before the open high moor claims the moorland walker.

South of Roos, and nearer to the road, is the aptly named (28) GREAT STAPLE TOR 455m (543760). Very much the dominant tor in this group, its title has originated from the Anglo-Saxon word, 'staple' meaning a tower or steeple. This tor also provides numerous rock basins.

Continuing along the ridge, Great Staple has two further members of the family, the immediate neighbour being (29) MIDDLE STAPLE TOR 431m (541757), with LITTLE STAPLE TOR 380m midway between Middle Staple and the road.

Although not obviously quarried in the true sense of the word, much granite from the Staple Tors has been removed and used in the provision of Plymouth's pavement setts, still very much in use today. Also, it was granite taken from these tors that was used in the construction of Castle Drogo, near Drewsteignton, between 1911 and 1930.

Where Staple ridge descends towards the valley floor and road, the hamlet and quarry of Merrivale are to be found; this is the last remaining, working, granite quarry on Dartmoor.

Whilst driving between the car park previously mentioned, and Merrivale, a rather special tor, to the south and below road level, should be looked out for. Named (30) VIXEN TOR 317m (544743), it is not always very apparent in its

Vixen Tor

low position, but it is well worth looking out for. Known for its likeness to the shape of a capped head from certain angles, it is said to be the tallest tor on Dartmoor, with a height on the south side of 30 metres. Associated with this tor we have its own resident witch, known for luring unsuspecting travellers into the nearby Vixen Tor bog. Visitors beware!

Returning to the north side of the road, but on the opposite side of the valley to the Staple Tors above Merrivale, you will observe the mighty (31) GREAT MIS TOR 538m (563770). Its size and position make it visible from many vantage points along the road. The tor itself, on the crown of the hill, covers a large area and consists of widely separated stacks, the infilling granite now strewn in vast quantities, as clitter, on the valley side below. Great Mis Tor presents us with the largest example of a rock basin on the moor, privileged with its own title of 'The Devil's Pan'.

A word of caution should you decide to walk up to this tor. Great Mis lies just within the army live firing area. Should a red flag be flying from the tor, do NOT approach.

Coming back south from Great Mis and crossing the road, the tor which dominates this skyline is (16) NORTH HESSARY TOR 517m (578743). Not that it is the tor that dominates it is the T.V. transmission mast that pin-points a rather insignificant outcrop, a mast often wholly or partially obscured in mist. The tor is accessible from the road, with limited parking available, or by going on into Princetown and approaching from that direction. (See Two Bridges/Yelverton section on page 15).

Below North Hessary can be seen the two heavily quarried tors of (17) FOGGINTOR 400m (567736), and (18) SWELL TOR 400m (560733). (See Two Bridges/Yelverton section on page 15).

A third tor in this group, less eroded by quarrying activity, and closer to the road, is (32) KING'S TOR 390m (557738). On close observation it is possible to see signs of the route of the old Princetown/Yelverton railway line which wound its way around these tors. Sidings led off the line into the quarries allowing the easier removal of granite off the moor, en-route to destinations all over the country.

Great Mis Tor

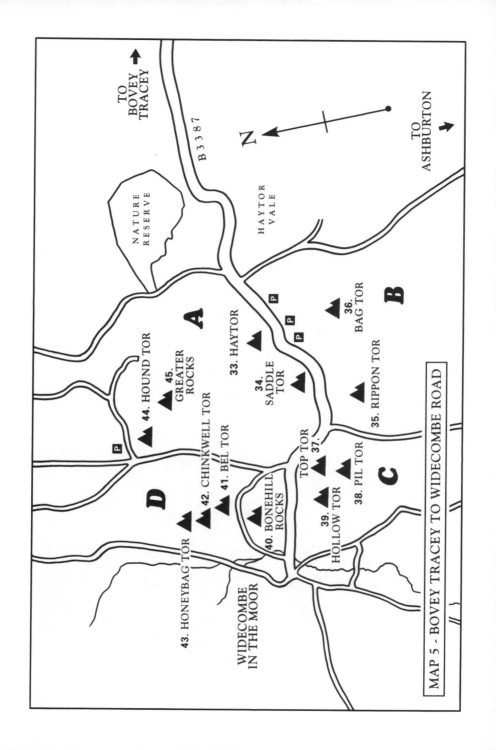

MAP 5 - BOVEY TRACEY TO WIDECOMBE ROAD

▬Tors along the Bovey Tracey/▬ Widecombe Road - map 5

MAP SECTION A.

From whichever direction you approach (33) HAYTOR 457m (757771), its name and shape has gone before it and therefore its identity is known to many. The name has derived from 'Hey', itself following on from 'High'.

Not that it is the highest tor, but without doubt it is the most conspicuous and well known tor in the area. Visible from many parts of South Devon and the sea, it is the most visited tor on Dartmoor.

Its magnetic popularity is of great concern to the National Park Authority and all lovers of Dartmoor, as the sensitive surrounding landscape, including the granite itself, is being seriously eroded by the myriad hands and feet which pour over this prominent point. The majesty of Haytor itself can be well observed from both road and neighboring tors, such as Rippon and Saddle; the desire to climb a tor 'because it is there' can be fulfilled by an assault on one of the many others that are also very accessible from the road.

The area of Haytor itself can also offer a wide range of fascinations for the inquisitive visitor whilst drinking in the ever-changing views of moor and South Devon way below, the disused quarries and granite railway being but two.

Haytor's neighbour to the west is (34) SADDLE TOR 428m (752764).

Saddle Tor

Lying within easy reach of the road and relevant car park, the height of this tor from the south looks insignificant. However, on its northern side the drop is more dramatic and the view very worthwhile. Access to the series of redundant quarries and their feeder granite tramways which are to be found on the northern flanks of Saddle Tor and Haytor can be made from here.

Both these tors are known as 'Avenue tors' describing the fact that they consist of two separate stacks with a dividing avenue between.

MAP SECTION B.

On the opposite (south side) of the road to Saddle Tor lies (35) RIPPON TOR 473m (747756). Strategically positioned with roads on two sides, Widecombe/Bovey to the north, Widecombe/Ashburton to the west. This less advertised high tor, gives superb views over the moor (including Haytor), and the South Devon countryside. In the days before cars and tourism the quietness of this place encouraged the nesting of Dartmoor ravens, the fact of which was recorded in the tor often being called 'Raven Tor'.

From Rippon's summit, looking east (and from various points along the road between Haytor and Rippon) can be seen the only other tor in this sector. (36) BAG TOR 349m (762757) is situated on the edge of the moorland ledge before it drops down to the softer South Devon cultivated lowland. Although a tor of considerable interest, access from the road is impeded in part by Bag Tor mire (marshland) and should not be attempted without appropriate footwear.

MAP SECTION C.

This section finds three independent tors all situated on the same hill formation to the south and west of the Widecombe hill road.

On the summit, aptly named, is (37) TOP TOR 432m (736763). Known locally as 'Tapter', this well fragmented pile contains one of the many logan stones found on the moor.

At a slightly lower altitude on the southern edge of this summit ridge lies (38) PIL TOR 420m (734759). Pil overlooks the remains of an ancient Iron Age farmstead, 'Foale's Arrishes', named after a later owner who used these earlier enclosures to enpound his livestock.

The third tor (39) HOLLOW TOR 370m (732763), is situated on the west facing slope of the hillside, below Pil and Top tors, overlooking Widecombe. Best seen from the road when climbing up out of the village.

MAP SECTION D.

In this section to the north of the road, and visible as the climb is made up Widecombe hill, are a group of four tors, situated along the ridge of the hill. Closest to the road is an outcrop known as (40) BONEHILL ROCKS 393m (732775). Easily reached by a loop lane running from the outskirts of Widecombe to the top of Widecombe hill.

To the north of both loop road and Bonehill is (41) BEL TOR 390m (731778). Here can be found some excellent examples of rock basins. Both these tors give superb views of Widecombe.

Continuing north and slightly below the summit ridge are (42) CHINKWELL TOR 390m (728780) and then finally, the colourfully named (43) HONEYBAG TOR 445m (728787), situated at the extremity of the ridge. Of the four tors in this group Honeybag is the most dramatic in size and structure.

Bonehill Rocks, Bel Tor, Chinkwell Tor and Honeybag Tor

MAP SECTION A.

Before leaving the tors associated with this road we return to Section A for two tors, which although visible from the Bovey/Widecombe road, require a detour for closer inspection. Turn north along the Moretonhampstead road (see map) for some two miles and the magnificent **(44) GREAT HOUND TOR 414m (743790)** will come into view on the right. (Car park at first road junction).

Luck, for the motorist, would have it that this most noble tor would be within such easy reach of the road. Named after its seeming likeness to hounds overlooking a natural battlement, association with hounds both real and mystical are now tightly woven into the legend of this dramatic and beautiful place. It was apt that some of the shooting for a B.B.C. production of *The Hound of The Baskervilles* was carried out in this area.

From Great Hound Tor, looking in a south easterly direction, some $\frac{1}{2}$ mile distant, can be seen **(45) GREAT (Grea) TOR 371m (747787)**; very much a natural rampart of granite, situated on the very edge of the valley dividing Hound Tor and Haytor Downs.

Should you consider a walk from Hound to Great Tor, at the bottom of the dip between the two, you will find the fascinating remains of a medieval village, once a thriving community.

▰▰▰ *Tors along the Tavistock/* ▰▰▰ *Okehampton Road - map 6*

The Tavistock/Okehampton road, the A386, runs close to the western boundary of Dartmoor (north of Lydford it actually is the National Park Boundary for some distance). Due to this geographical fact all the tors lie to the east of the road, except one.

To begin with we will concentrate on the majority, all bar one being well set back from the road, making an impressive backcloth, especially with the late afternoon sun illuminating them.

Nearest to Okehampton and first visible from the road at the A30 roundabout, situated at the west end of the by-pass, the highest peak in Southern England is briefly visible. This is (46) HIGH WILLHAY 621m (580895). To its left (north) in close company is YES TOR 619m. Both tors are situated within the army live firing area but can be approached along the army track from the Okehampton Battle Camp site as long as the red flags are NOT flying.

Having turned off the A30 onto the A386, the small village of Sourton indicates the immediate position of (47) SOURTON TORS 440m (543898), situated above the village. Should you wish to climb a tor on this route this will be your best bet if time is limited. Although a steep climb up from the little car park in front of the church, the distance is short and the view can be spectacular.

The stretch of road between Sourton and the turning down to Lydford does not allow much of a view of the moor, nor are there really any safe options for parking. Near to the Lydford turning a stop for refreshment at one of two inns will allow you to view the tors in the immediate vicinity.

To your front, and most easily identified is (48) BRAT (or Brai) TOR 452m (540857). Situated a mile from the road this tor is crowned with a granite cross. Erected on the instruction of William Widgery, a well-known Dartmoor and Exmoor artist, and named after him, the cross celebrated Queen Victoria's Golden Jubilee in 1887.

Straddling Brat Tor are two small tors; to the north (49) ARMS TOR 457m (542863), to the south (50) DOE TOR 425m (543848). These three tors, all in the army live firing area, are situated on the flanks of the western moor, below the summit plateau.

Positioned on this summit, overlooking their smaller brethren below are (51)

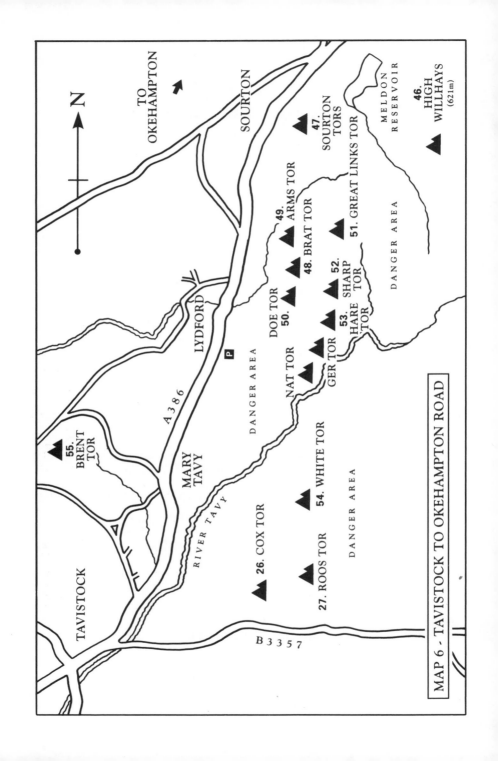

MAP 6 - TAVISTOCK TO OKEHAMPTON ROAD

GREAT LINKS TOR 586m (552867). A magnificent, fortress like structure, its high, strategic position provides views over a vast area of Dartmoor, Devon and Cornwall. South of Great Links then comes (52), another SHARP TOR 519m (550848), with finally in this group, (53) HARE TOR 531m (552843), standing as northern marker to the north moor's gorge, known as Tavy Cleave.

The inaccessibility and distance of these tors from the road do not make them sensible objectives for the unprepared walker.

A section of road from a mile south of the Lydford turning to Mary Tavy, crosses open moorland. As you enter this area from the Okehampton direction, having first crossed the cattle grid, an army road turning, uphill, with car parking, allows plenty of room to stop and look back at the tors just mentioned.

As the road crosses this piece of open moorland the distant tors are hidden from view, only reappearing as Mary Tavy is approached. Once again, stopping on this rather fast section of road is not easy. From the area above the old winding house of Wheal Betsy, a redundant lead and silver mine, it is possible to look across the intervening valleys to the distant tors beyond.

Hound Tor

Three miles away, on the far side of the River Tavy, stands (54) WHITE TOR 468m (543787), as the northern (left) sentinel of a group of tors.

Individual identification of these tors is not easy as perspective and distance are hard to assess. The right-hand marker is (26) COX TOR 442m (531762). These two tors on the wings stand forward of (27) ROOS TOR 454m (543767) and (28) GREAT STAPLE TOR 455m (543760), Great Staple being tucked in behind to the left of Cox Tor. Further back still and to the right of White Tor is (31) GREAT MIS TOR 538m (563770), some five miles distant from this road.

You will realize that the relative positions of these tors will change as your position on the road changes. An interesting exercise in observation and map-reading ! For information on these last four tors see the Two Bridges/Tavistock section (see page 21).

In conclusion we return to the one exception, the one tor to the west of the road. Visible as you cover the section of road across open moor, (55) BRENT TOR 310m (474805) is unusual in more than one way. On its summit is the small church of St Michael, built in the 12th century. Visible from the Bristol Channel on clear days, it was used as a navigational aid for sailors in days gone by. Brent Tor is also unusual in that it is constructed of volcanic lava, not being part of the Dartmoor granite mass. A car park is provided at the base of the tor for the use of visitors.

A
Glimpse of
DARTMOOR
PLACE NAMES

Andrew Stevens

Peninsula
Press

The map of Dartmoor on pages 16-17 is reproduced with the kind permission of the Dartmoor National Park Authority.

Line drawings by Sue Capey.
Other illustrations by Brian Ainsworth.

Published by Peninsula Press Ltd
P.O. Box 31
Newton Abbot
Devon TQ12 5XH

Tel: 0803 875875

Printed in England by D.D.S. Colour Printers, Weston-Super-Mare.

ISBN 1 872640 09 5

A GLIMPSE OF DARTMOOR
· PLACE NAMES ·

Contents

Introduction 4

Common Elements 5

Alphabetical list of place names 10

Map of Dartmoor 16

Books 32

Introduction

Dartmoor was given National Park status in 1951. This area included the ancient Forest of Dartmoor and the surrounding border parishes with their common lands. The title 'Forest' therefore, is not a reference to trees, because, although more wooded than at present, (discounting Forestry Commission conifer plantations), it was never a true forest. It is called Forest because of its status from the 13th century as a Royal hunting ground. Strictly speaking, when King Henry III gave the area to his brother Richard in 1239, it automatically became a 'chase' technically, because a Forest could only be possessed by the sovereign. Richard was then only the Duke of Cornwall, and since that time, Dartmoor has largely remained Duchy property - even if the title of Forest has persisted.

The place names of Dartmoor are mainly of Saxon origin because, in most areas, there was some time between the withdrawal of the Celts and takeover by the Saxons. As a result, only some of the Celtic names survived. The names of many physical locations are relatively recent. Virtually every landmark, however small, has a name as a reference point for knowing where you are and for giving directions to someone else.

Obviously there are altogether too many place names to explain without exception, and besides, it is often possible to work out probable derivations once certain common elements are known and some likely sources investigated in examples.

Map references such as Tavy Cleave (SX 5583) mostly refer to the Ordnance Survey Outdoor Leisure map 28 which covers the whole of the National Park using the scale 2½ inches to 1 mile (4cm to 1km). SX is the area grid reference.

The Author

Andrew Guy Stevens was born in Crewkerne, Somerset in 1945. He is the grandson of Philip Guy Stevens whose ink drawings illustrated William Crossing's famous *Guide to Dartmoor*. His early love of the moor was nurtured through annual family holidays which included marathon walks with Eric Hemery, author of *High Dartmoor*. He moved to Devon in 1979 and is currently Head of the Music Department at St Thomas' High School in Exeter.

◆

Common Elements

The River Dart which gives its name to the area is a Celtic word meaning Oak, and if you go to Wistman's Wood (SX 61 77) on the West Dart, or Dartmeet (SX 67 73), where the East and West Dart meet, the name makes obvious sense.

Short names, many of the rivers for example, have simple Celtic or Anglo-Saxon origins, but these and other ancient words are frequently combined to produce the place names that we find on modern maps. However, it must be said that change is a continuous process, and there are many place names on current Ordnance Survey maps which are different from the names in use ninety or a hundred years ago.

Obviously a knowledge of local social, religious and industrial history will help unravel the origins and meanings of place names: several authors have already done this most thoroughly (see page 32). And so, armed with some information and a little imagination, you can turn research back on itself so to speak and develop some insight into the history of the places you visit and the features you may observe, whether by choice or by chance.

One technique that might be useful if you are on your own or with 'understanding' friends, is to say the place names, with and without a Devon accent, and thereby appreciate how spoken sounds may change through useage and eventually lead to their being written differently. For example, the current word for boulder debris covering the slopes of a tor is CLITTER. Originally it was CLATTER. The local accent tends to soften the first vowel sound in this case.

BALL - often in the name of a hill which has a distinctly rounded shape.

BARTON - principal farm of a group in that it provided a central store, for barley in particular. Often known as the 'home farm' and frequently an enclosed design with a gated archway into the central yard.

BEACON - there are several hills on Dartmoor which incorporate this term. Some imply their earlier use as places where beacon fires were lit owing to their prominence, but others are probably derived from other local place names. For example, Ugborough Beacon (SX 66 59), might have been Peak Down Hill or Picken Hill originally.

BEAM - this always has some mining significance, either directly to deep, open workings where beam engines would have operated the mining equipment, or later on, to the adjacent hills.

BEARE or BERE - occasional association with the meaning 'fortified place' (Old English - *burh*), but more usually a reference to a wooded area of some sort.

BLACK - a very common component in place names, but not as obvious in meaning as might at first appear. The Anglo-Saxon word *blaec* means pale or colourless and both black and bleak are derived from this word. Bleak tends to imply the pale desolation of exposed hillsides whereas black implies the dark appearance of shaded valleys or woodland. Thus the two extremes of colourless can be interpreted.

BUCKLAND - common throughout Devon, this is a corruption of 'book land' and implies that the land was registered as being held by Royal Charter, dating from Saxon times.

COOMBE or COMBE or COMB - from the Celtic word *cym* which means a small valley usually closed at its upper end. The change to 'cum' or 'cam' is obvious but to 'ham' less so. Birkham Gate (SX 57 67) is not named on any map but it is also known as Burracombe Gate. With Burrator close-by, the whole area might have been known as Burra- or Bearacombe which simply means 'wooded valley'- which is what it is.

CLEAVE - as in Tavy Cleave (SX 55 83); in other words the valley through which the river Tavy flows, but since the word is probably derived from the Anglo-Saxon *cleof* meaning cliff, it describes the steep sides of the valley rather than the valley itself.

-DON - is simply a shortened version of 'down', but since 'don' and 'ton' sound almost identical as endings to longer place names, it is not surprising that the two versions have come to mean the some thing in some cases. For example Skerraton (SX 70 64) was *Sciredon* in records dating back to the 13th century. There are many examples of tautology in place-names, which have developed through time, and nearby Skerraton Down is just such a case. (Coombe Valley, just north of Bude in Cornwall, is a perfect example of this.)

FORD - implies a way of some sort, often across a river or stream, but not necessarily so. Sandy Ford, on the ancient burial path (Lich or Lynch Way) from Postbridge to the nearest Parish Church at Lydford, is devoid of river crossings. It is not marked on any maps, but the path descends through Sandy Ford to Hill Bridge (SX 53 80) from White Barrow (SX 56 79) between Langstone Moor and the newtake walls to the North. (see also WORTHY).

-HAM - one of several part-words indicating farm, homestead or nucleated village. This useage tends to be more common as you go south. Indeed the whole of the area to the south-east of Dartmoor is known as the South Hams.

LAKE - areas of standing water are always known as 'pools' on Dartmoor, whereas 'lake' refers to a small contributary stream. Dead Lake (SX 56 78) is a typical example. So is Red Lake (SX 64 66) although it should be noted that the 'pool' that is obvious in that area is the result of comparatively recent china clay workings.

-LEIGH (LEY) - this suffix refers to a woodland setting, or rather a natural clearing in woodland.

NEWTAKE - originally there were 35 ancient tenement farms that lay within the bounds of the Forest. There were certain rights attached to these tenements, including the right to enclose up to eight acres of land. These rights continued up to 1796, but since then a great deal of moorland, including common land, has been enclosed regardless of 'rights'. All such enclosures, old and new, are generally known as 'newtakes'.

POUND - usually a reference to a Bronze Age settlement where a roughly circular wall enclosed an area where both humans and their animals were at least partially protected. Therefore it is normal to find hut circles and other evidence of human habitation within the pound wall. DRIFT POUNDS were different in that they were enclosures constructed solely for the purpose of empounding cattle after they had been rounded up from the open moor.

STOCK - from the old English word *stoc* means 'secondary settlement', implying a farm other than the home or Barton Farm. Thus Tavistock would simply be 'farm on the River Tavy'. The fact that there was an abbey at Tavistock and that the old English word for 'holy place' was 'stow' might be confusing at first glance. The town is outside the National Park boundaries, but has great significance to Dartmoor in mining terms, since it was one of the four stannary towns where ore from the mines was brought to be weighed and stamped.

-TON - simply denotes 'farm' or 'enclosed area', but nothing in terms of size to the present-day derivative 'town'.

WELL - this word was sometimes used to describe natural springs, the only true well on the open moor being Fitz or Fitz's Well (SX 59 93).

WARREN - there are several place names incorporating this word; e.g. Hentor Warren (SX 59 65) and Ditsworthy Warren (SX 58 67). In each case this refers to the systematic management of rabbits for food, in comparatively recent times. The warrener would build large banks of stones and earth covered in turf to encourage the wild rabbit population to colonise. There are several ruins of the warreners' houses to be seen as additional evidence of these enterprises.

-WORTHY - from the Anglo-Saxon for 'enclosed homestead'. However there the simplicity ends because, of all the components of Dartmoor place names, this has evolved the most variants, including -ary, -ery, -over, -iver, -ever, even to -ford. North Hessary Tor above Princetown (SX 57 74), was more commonly known as Hisworthy Tor as recently as the beginning of the twentieth century.

Wheal Betsy, Mary Tavy. The engine house of what was once the most important lead and silver mine on Dartmoor, now owned by the National Trust

Alphabetical list of place names

ABBOTT'S WAY - (SX 68 65 and 61 67). There is an Abbey at Buckfast and there was one at Tavistock. Certainly the monks would have walked from one to the other, but whether they were responsible for the track in the first place is doubtful. The route is at least partially marked by crosses, although it is not certain that these were erected by the monks. SIWARD'S CROSS, better known as NUN'S CROSS (SX 60 69), is perhaps the best known of these, but there is evidence to suggest that this had been set up as a boundary rather than way marker and that 'Nun' is a corruption of its 17th century name *Nannecross. Nans* was a Celtic word for valley or dale.

Siward's (Nun's) Cross

ASHBURTON - (SX 75 69). Ash is a tree; burn is a stream; and ton is a homestead. From its origins as 'a small settlement by the stream where ash trees grow', it grew to become one of the principal towns serving the Dartmoor mining industry. Indeed it became one of the four stannary towns and there were important tracks to it from Plymouth and Tavistock, which were marked with guide-stones.

AVON - (SX 65 69). From the Celtic word meaning 'river'. Several place names off the moor incorporate its name as a locational reference.

BEARDOWN MAN - (SX 59 79). This is one of Dartmoor's tallest 'menhirs' or standing stones. 'Man' probably comes from the Celtic word *maen* meaning 'stone', but could simply be that such a stone looks like a figure, seen from a distance against the sky. Beardown ought to mean 'wooded hill', and Beardown

Tors are a little to the south and above Wistman's Wood which, at one time, was considerably more extensive.

BELLEVER - (SX 65 77). There is a tor, an ancient tenement farm and a well-known clapper bridge, each bearing this name. In early Duchy records the name was Welford which would seem to refer to the river crossing. There were several later corruptions of this; Wellaford (1579): Bellabur (1608); Bellaford (1663); and Bellefor (1736). William Crossing was using the 1663 spelling in his *Guide to Dartmoor* which was first published in 1909. I'm told that there is still a road-sign with this spelling in the area!

Clapper Bridge at Bellever, 1910

BELSTONE - (SX 62 93). If you believed the article in the *Western Morning News* during 1890, then you would be of the opinion that this name refers to a stone dedicated to the Phoenician god Baal! In Doomsday however, the place was recorded as *Bellestham*. *Belles* was a common name at that time and the terminal 'ham' can refer to an adjacent river bend, but more commomly simply means 'enclosure'. However, the English Place Name Society has the Doomsday spelling as *Bellestam* - a compound of two Old English words *belle* and *stan*, meaning the bell stone. This was supposed to make reference to '...a remarkably fine logan rock that rolled like a ship in a gale.' (*Little Guide Series*, Devon, 1900).

BITTAFORD - SX (66 57). The 'ford' is self-explanatory, but I can find no explanation of 'Bitta-'. It is not a reference to a river name, since the ford (and well-known bridge) is across the Lud Brook. It is probably another example of a personal name becoming part of a place name.

BOWERMAN'S NOSE - (SX 74 80). This massive granite pile of rocks, over thirty feet in height, has weathered in such a way that, from a distance, it can resemble a human profile. There are several stories about the origin of the name, but none has been properly substantiated. All that really matters is to make the distinction between this natural formation that suggests human characteristics, and the standing stones and crosses on Dartmoor which people have erected to serve some purpose or other.

BLACKINGSTONE ROCK - (SX 78 85). Probably this was originally just Blackstone, - which is self explanatory; thence via the pronunciation Blackystone to the current spelling. The 'Rock' part is superfluous. Legend has it that this and the other similar neighbouring rock piles were formed when King Arthur and the Evil One threw quoits at each other in battle, the missiles changing to rocks as they landed!

BRENT TOR - (SX 47 80). This is well outside the perimeter of the National Park, but it is a tor (with a church on top) and typifies the useage of the word 'brent' meaning 'prominent'.

BUCKFASTLEIGH - (SX 73 66). This is a compound of three Old English words; *buc* meaning 'deer', *feasten* meaning 'stronghold', and *leah* meaning 'clearing in the thicket'. Deer on Dartmoor were hunted to extinction by 1780, although they have recently recolonised some of the wooded valleys surrounding the moor, the Teign valley in particular.

BURRATOR WATERFALL - (SX 55 67). This is situated in the ancient woodland below the reservoir dam. The whole area was probably known as *Beara-*, *Bira-*, or *Burra-combe*, meaning 'wooded valley'. The -tor is really the high ground above. The more obvious waterfall (SX 55 68) is marked 'fall' on the map and is man-made. The Devonport Leat was originally constructed as a water supply for the Devonport area of Plymouth. When the original dam was opened in 1898, the lower section of the leat became redundant and the water was simply piped from its course along Yennadon Down and emptied into the reservoir.

CADOVER BRIDGE -(SX 55 64). The origins of this name go back to at least the 13th century. Cadworthy Farm has been so-called since this time, and the adjacent bridge was known as *Pontem de Cadaworth* in 1408. It is thought that the River Plym (hence Plymouth) was originally called the Cad. The river is easily fordable here, hence the suffix 'over' or 'way over the Cad'.

CATOR-(SX 68 76). Originally *Cadatrea* (1167), this is another place name that incorporates a person's name, in this case it is Cada's tree. According to a forester's account five hundred years ago, two of the five *villes* in the parish of Widecombe were the 'hamlet of North Catrowe' and the 'villat of Higher Catrowe'. The *venvilles* were the farms on the outskirts of the moor that, on payment of a small annual fee or *fin ville*, had commoners' rights on the adjacent moor, (usually of pasturage and turbary; i.e. grazing and peat cutting). Where a tree is part of a place name, it usually holds some special significance as a meeting place.

CHAGFORD -(SX 70 87). *Chag* is an Old English dialect word for gorse or broom and only found in place name compounds. With reference to '-ford', there are two ancient bridges over the River Teign at Chagford and stepping stones at Rushford Mill Farm just outside (SX 70 88). Chagford was another of the four principal stannary towns in the 14th century. (For a fuller explanation, see *Crossing's Guide to Dartmoor* pages 34-35.)

CHALLACOMBE - (SX 69 79). Also spelt Chalnecombe until recently and derived from the 14th century *Chelvecombe*, or 'valley of calves'. This was another of the venville farms. (see **CATOR**, and, for a fuller account, refer to *Crossing's Guide to Dartmoor*, pages 38-39.)

CHILDE'S TOMB - (SX 62 70). 'Cild' was a common Saxon appellation, and *Childe* a title of honour in the Middle Ages, but the story, or rather, legend associated with this Christian cross set beside a pagan kist and surrounded by a stone circle , was documented by Risdon nearly four hundred years ago, but is still popular myth. Childe the Hunter was caught in a blizzard and in a futile attempt to save himself, sacrificed his horse, disembowelled it and sheltered in the warm carcass! (see *Place Names of Plymouth, Dartmoor and the Tamar Valley* by W. Best Harris for a more comprehensive account.)

COSDON HILL - (SX 63 91). In the 1240 survey of Dartmoor known as the Perambulation, the name was *Cossdonne* - a compound of the personal name *Cos(s)* and *don(ne)* meaning 'hill'. Local pronunciation of the word is 'Cosson'. Between 1888 and the 1986, Ordnance Survey maps have incorrectly used the name 'Cawsand', but the recent Outdoor Leisure edition has reverted to the correct spelling.

CRANMEER POOL - (SX 60 85). One of the best known place names on Dartmoor, partly because of its bleak remoteness (even if approached by the military road from Okehampton), and more recently because it is the site of one of the original 'letter-boxes'. Indeed, its housing is really the only feature of the place since there's precious little pool any more. Until the recent craze for 'letter-boxing'- following clues and sampling the rubber stamps - the idea was to achieve the remote location, (Fur Tor -SX 58 83, and Duck's Pool -SX 62 67 are two other such places) and leave a stamped postcard in the letter-box for the next visitor to collect and post. Originally the name was *Crau Meer* meaning 'lake of the Crows'.

Saracen's Head Inn, 1797

DREWSTEIGNTON - (SX 73 90). Drew, as a family name can be traced back to 1210 in its original form *Drogo*. So the modern name is simply 'Drew's farm by the River Teign'. Nearby Castle Drogo became the most recent family home when it was completed in 1930. Until very recently, when the National Trust took over much of the estate, the family continued to own property in the village and in Broadhembury to the east (SX 10 04). Both villages have inns called the 'Drewe Arms'.

DRIZZLECOMBE - (SX 58 66). According to Crossing in 1909, Drizzle is a vernacular corruption of 'Thrushel'. Crossing refers to an old map in his possession which uses this name, although he recognises that the Ordnance Survey maps of the time were using 'Drizzle'. The location is important as one of the richest sites on Dartmoor for ancient relics, including fine stone rows and a great menhir (standing stone), all of which had become prostrate, but were re-erected in July 1893.

ERME - (SX 62 66). An interesting river name in as much as that the town Ermington probably gave its name to the river rather than the other way round. This, like the Plym, is known as 'back formation'. The Old English word *iermen* means 'main' or 'principal', so Ermington would have been the most important farm in the area (SX 63 53).

FERNWORTHY - (SX 66 84). It seems that 'fern' is a reference to bracken, which is the commonest type of fern and abundant on Dartmoor. Originally, Fernworthy was a group of three small farms with enclosures: now it is a reservoir surrounded by a large conifer plantation! In years of severe drought, it is possible to cross the South Teign by Fernworthy Bridge or the adjacent single stone clapper bridge, and thereby complete the ancient way from Metherall (SX 67 83) through Fernworthy to Froggymead (SX 65 84).

FINGLE BRIDGE - (SX 74 89). This narrow, three-arched structure is the old pack-horse way across the River Teign, and so-named because the Fingle brook enters the river immediately downstream. The modern spelling seems to date back to 1765, and the name had probably developed from the Old English word *fang* which meant to 'hold or catch'; which might suggest that the location was known for its fishing. Of course, it is cars which attempt the crossing now to the parking facilities beyond (most of them successfully), for the area has become a popular so-called 'beauty spot'. Incidentally, the 'V' shaped recesses which form part of the parapet, were designed to 'streamline' the structure in times of exceptional flood.

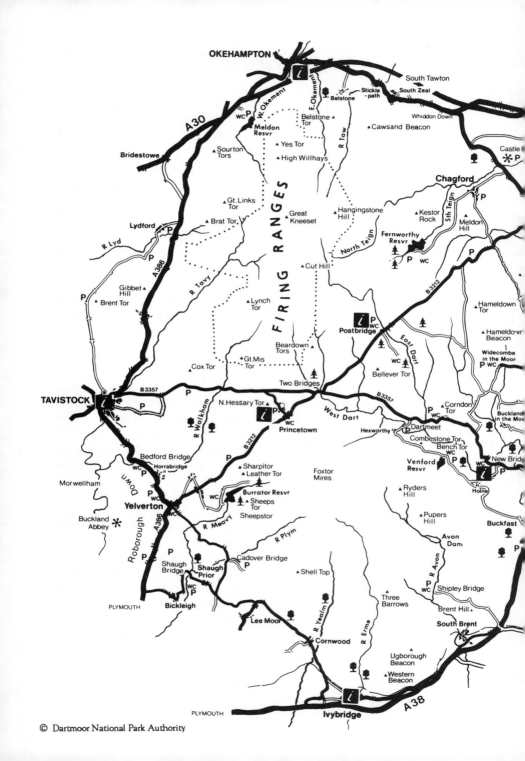

© Dartmoor National Park Authority

DARTMOOR

EXETER
A30

R Telgn

Dunsford
Steps Bridge
P WC *i*

Bridford

▲ Blackingstone Rock

etonhampstead

Christow

Kennick
Trenchford
& Tottiford
Resvrs

Hennock

Lustleigh
Becky Falls

HQ *i*

**Bovey
Tracey**

WC
P   Ilsington

A38

NEWTON ABBOT

NEWTON ABBOT

ASHBURTON

STLEIGH

OTNES & TORBAY

n

| 1 | 2 | 3 | 4 | 5 | miles |

| 2 | 3 | 4 | 5 | kilometres |

These days they perform a useful function as escape bays from the 'stream' of vehicles negotiating the bridge!

GIDLEIGH - (SX 67 88). Literally 'Gydda's clearing'. Although there is no person of this name on record, various spellings of the place name date back to the 12th century. William Crossing makes reference to the 14th century castle, and wonders at what period the Gidleys came into possession of the nearby manor.

GREY WEATHERS - (SX 70 80). Much research has been done on these two fine stone circles on the side of Sittaford Tor, before and after their partial restoration, but only Burnard in 1890 makes any reference to the meaning of their name. He says that they are "...thus named from their fancied resemblance to a flock of sheep."

GRIMSPOUND - (SX 70 80). This is probably the most visited and best preserved Bronze Age enclosure on the moor. There are no references to its name until the end of the 18th century, but 'Grim' in several other place name contexts is always a reference to the Devil, and suggests that the Saxons associated such a large prehistoric settlement with diabolic forces.

HARFORD - (SX 63 59). In 1086, the name was Hereford. The Old English word *here* meant 'army', and *har* must be a corruption of this. Unless the name goes back to some confrontation between the Celts and the invading Saxon forces, the 'army' reference cannot be explained. The bridge at Harford is over the River Erme.

HARFORD BRIDGE - (SX 50 76), is over the River Tavy above Tavistock and has a different derivation, being a shortening of the earlier spelling 'Hartforde', and being a possible reference to the spot being a place where deer would cross the river.

HEXWORTHY - (SX65 72). The '-worthy' as usual implies an enclosed homestead, and the 'Hex' is a shortening of the personal name *Hexta* or *Hexte*; (15th century) - originally *Hexten*.

HOLNE - (SX 70 69).The name simply means 'place abounding in holly'. Certainly the area is wooded and the village feels sheltered. The fine church once belonged to Buckfast Abbey. The Church House Inn has a lengthy history as well, and there is a gravestone in the churchyard dedicated to Edward Collins, one time landlord of the inn, who died in December 1780. The inscription reads:

> *Here lies Poor Old Ned,*
> *On his last Mattrass bed,*
> *During life he was honest and free*
> *He knew well the Chace*
> *But has now run his Race*
> *And his name was COLLINS D'ye fee.*

HORRABRIDGE - (SX 51 69). Although Horrabridge is now a small town, it is the actual bridge over the River Walkham that is significant. 'Horra' is derived from the word *har*, meaning 'boundary', and the bridge is at the boundary of three parishes. Indeed there is a boundary stone on the bridge itself, set into the central parapet, facing downstream.

HUCCABY - (SX 66 72/3) Some of the early versions of this name perhaps provide a clue as to the original meaning: 1296 - *la Woghebye*; 1317 - *Woghby*: 1340 - *Woghebi*: 1417 - *Hogheby*: 1608 - *Hookeby*. The Old English word *woh* meant 'crooked' and *byge* meant 'bend ' or 'curve'. Certainly there is a big loop in the West Dart River here, separating Hexworthy from Huccaby on the other bank. However, Crossing points out that on the Hexworthy side of the river are some old farm enclosures know as the Byes,and notes that the '-by' in Huccaby is pronounced the same way by the locals; (rather than '-bee'). You have to draw your own conclusions in this case!

LETTAFORD - (SX 70 84). The Old English word *hluttor* meant 'clear, pure, bright', and so it would seem to indicate a crossing place of the stream at this point.

LUSTLEIGH - (SX 78 81). The English Place Name Society can only suggest that 'Lust-' is a derivative of the nickname *Luvesta* meaning 'dearest one', the '-leigh' as usual meaning 'clearing'. The community is outside the Dartmoor venville (see page 13, **CATOR** and *Crossing's Guide to Dartmoor* pages 38-39), but well within the National Park boundary and popular as a charming village in its own right and for its local scenery, in particular LUSTLEIGH CLEAVE which is the steep-sided ridge separating the Wray valley from the Bovey.

LYDFORD - (SX 51 84). Literally 'way over the river Lyd'. The river name has evolved from *aqua de Lide* (1249), through *Lidde* (1577) to its present form. It means 'noisy, loud stream' and certainly lives up to its name as it forces a way through Lydford Gorge. The Parish of Lydford is the largest in England, over 60,000 acres, including the whole of Dartmoor Forest, as fixed in the perambulation of 1240, and remaining practically unaltered to this day. Lydford was once the stronghold of King Alfred against the Danes, hence the castle, now in ruins. More recently, the village was served by two railway lines: the G.W.R single-track branch line from Plymouth, Marsh Mills to Launceston; and the S.R. double-track, Plymouth - Exeter - Waterloo main line. There are several road bridges left as evidence and a fine arched viaduct hidden away just to the east of the village (SX 514 846). The platforms of the combined station are overgrown but intact, and the site, undisturbed since 1968, has become a perfect and peaceful nature reserve.

MANATON - (SX 74 81). *Maene* was an Old English word meaning 'general' or 'common', and as part of a place name probably refered to an object that belonged to the whole community, or to a boundary marker that was common to adjacent estates.

MEAVY - (SX 54 67). The village simply takes its name from the river on which it stands. The name itself, also spelt Mewey, might well be pre-English, although the compound of Old English *maew* and *ie* would translate as 'Sea-gull river'. Close to the church gate is the famous ancient hollow oak tree, now supported and slowly dying; and underneath, the cross, which having been lost for over a century, was replaced on its pedestal (or calvary) and more recently restored. Don't be confused by the existence of a second large oak tree; that only goes back as far as 1918, the granite war memorial having been placed alongside a year later.

MELDON - (SX 55 92). The '-don' of Meldon is not a problem, but the 'Mel-' is!. The Old English adjective *maele* means 'spotted' or 'variagated': the old Celtic *mailo* means 'bare' or 'bald': and then *Maela* was also a personal name. Take your

Meavy, 1890, from Robert Burnard's *Dartmoor Pictorial Records*

Meavy, *c* 1954

pick! The English Place Name Society (*The Place Names of Devon* - Part 1, pages 203-204) discusses the derivation at some length without really coming to any firm conclusion. That apart, the actual hamlet of Meldon is tiny and the name these days is more usually used with reference to the huge quarry above the hamlet where vast quantities of stone are produced as track ballast for British Rail. The railhead for this operation is actually on the viaduct which crosses the Okement ravine, although no locomotives or loaded wagons may use the track. Further up the valley is the concrete dam of Dartmoor's newest and most controversial reservoir.

MERRIVALE - (SX 54 75). This name means 'pleasant, open space'. Indeed, there is precious little habitation here, apart from the Dartmoor Inn and the last working granite quarry on the moor. The name is also used to indicate one of the Army firing ranges in the area to the north, and the term 'Merrivale Antiquities' refers collectively to the abundant Bronze Age remains in evidence nearby. (SX 55 74).

MORETONHAMPSTEAD - (SX 75 86). In the Doomsday Book of 1086, the place is recorded as *Morton*, which is obviously 'moor farm'. The evolution to Moreton- is understandable, but there seems to be no explanation of the suffix 'hampstead', although the word is derived from the Saxon *ham-stede*, the place of the house. Indeed, the original two-syllable version is often used locally, and it would assist local road sign writers considerably if this version were revived officially!

OKEHAMPTON - (SX 58 95). This town is situated on the edge of the moor where main road and railway seem determined to squeeze a passage around the northern perimeter, at a point where the West and East Okement Rivers join. Of course the town takes its name from the rivers. In 1244 the river name was *aqua de Okem*, and *Ockment* by 1577. The first part of the name is from the Celtic *aku* meaning 'swift'. The second part may be derived from the Old Welsh *myned* - 'to go', or from the Aryan word *mim* meaning 'noisy'. Either way the picture of a fast flowing river is clear: indeed, both East and West Okements do descend rapidly from the high moor. It is interesting to note that the 1885 Ordnance Survey of Dartmoor uses the current spelling of the river name - OKEment - whereas writers of that period and for some time after were still using the old spelling - OCKment. The terminal '-hampton' is quite common and eventually replaced the Doomsday version *Ockmentune* or 'farm on the river Ockment'. Incidentally, 'Ockington', the local spoken corruption of the place name, has survived to this day.

PETER (MARY) TAVY - (SX 53 77 and 50 79). Although neither of these villages is actually adjacent to the River Tavy, they are close enough to have adopted the river name, combined with the names of the Saints to which their churches are dedicated. In each case the two elements should be pronounced as one word with the first element accented.

POSTBRIDGE - (SX 58 73). The 'clapper' bridge at Postbridge is probably the best known of its type on the moor, mainly because of its accessibility. The suffix 'Post' probably only dates back as far as the construction of the three-arched road bridge alongside. This new bridge would have been an important link in establishing the post-road from Moretonhampstead.These days, the garage and store close by the bridge also doubles as the local Post Office, and it was from there, right into the middle 1960's, that Mr Jack Bellamy would deliver the post on horseback - the last mounted postman in the country. Jack's son Reg, who has maintained his links with the village, recalls hearing the supporting piles of stones in the clapper bridge itself refered to as 'pawsts', and certainly this would be the pronounciation of 'post' with a broad Devon accent.

Postbridge, 1889

PRINCETOWN - (SX 58 73). This is a comparatively new settlement and developed around the notorious prison which was built between 1805 and 1809 to house French and American prisoners of war. A simple explanation of the name would be to accept that it was an association with the Prince Regent, afterwards George 1V. However, William Crossing, who, at the turn of the century, had several connections with the people of the town, did not accept such a straightforward explanation. PRINCE HALL (SX 62 74), now a Hotel, was formerly one of the ancient tenements mentioned in the earliest Forest records. At about the same time that Sir Thomas Tyrwhitt was building a large residence for himself at TOR ROYAL (SX 69 78), a Judge Buller had acquired Prince Hall for development. He was also responsible for extending and developing TWO BRIDGES (SX 60 75), adding some cottages and the Saracen's Head Inn. When Arthur Young, the authority on agriculture, visited the area in 1796 he made reference to Two Bridges as Princetown. Quite apart from this, the prison site was always known as Dartmoor Prison and this is confirmed, for example, in a letter written by an official of the Transport Board in 1805, in which there is no reference to the prison site being at Princetown. Thus Crossing was suggesting that the name had been transferred from the developing community at Two Bridges. Either way, the prison town did acquire its current name, whatever its origin, and this is confirmed by an indisputable reference in the baptismal register (1812):-

> 'October 4th Ann, *daughter of William Robins and Ann his wife,*
> *resident at Prince Town Brewery.'*

After this date, the place name often appears in this register, although it seems that it was not more generally used for some time.

Prince Hall, 1797, from an 18th century water colour

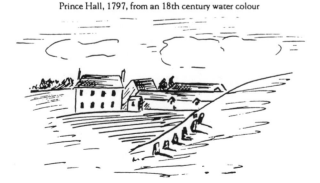

RUNDLESTONE - (SX 57 74). According to William Crossing, this small collection of buildings, high up on the road between Two Bridges and Tavistock, takes its name from the granite pillar, the Rundle Stone, that once marked the Royal Forest boundary. It had been recognised as such in 1702, although it had not been mentioned in surveys of the area prior to this date. The stone stood on the south side of the road immediately opposite the more recent Lydford/Walkhampton parish boundary-stone. Crossing measured the stone in 1881:

> 'It stood 7 feet above the stones in which it was set, and was four feet in girth. Near the top was the letter R cut in relief. It is marked on a map dated 1720 as a "Great Stone call'd Roundle."'

(The stone was broken up some years after 1881 to provide building material for a nearby wall.)

Hansford Worth, however, writing some 40 years later, challenges Crossing's explanation. In particular, he notes that, apart from Nun's Cross (SX 60 69), all the Forest Boundary markers were natural objects and that the so-called Rundle Stone was not strictly on the line of the boundary anyway. Worth takes up the 'roundle' version of the word. In everyday parlance and in heraldry, it means 'small circular object'. He suggests that nearby Rundlestone Tor (SX 57 74) which is on the Forest Boundary line, is the real Roundle Stone - especially because of its unique rock-basins. One of these 'roundles' was formed before the whole main slab moved from a level position, allowing a second basin to form near the summit on the new level surface. He concludes - "This rock, with its considerable area, its thickness of 4' 6", and the circles of its rock basins, certainly agrees with the description given in 1736 - 'a Great Stone call'd Roundle'." (Until the most recent revision of the Ordnance Survey maps, the place name had mysteriously been spelt Rendlestone for several decades.)

SAMPFORD SPINEY - (SX 53 72). This tiny village is just to the west of the river Walkham, the first part of the place name being a reference to the river crossing, a sandy ford, 'Samp-' being a corruption of the 1086 spelling *Sanford(a)*. Spiney refers to Gerard de Spineto who held the manor in the early 13th century.

SHAUGH PRIOR - (SX 54 63). Shaugh is a typical Dartmoor border settlement, with the buildings grouped around the solid old parish church. There have been several spellings and pronounciations of the name, all of which relate to the Old

English word *sceaga*, which means 'wooded', a description which certainly still applies today. The manor was from the earliest times owned by Plympton Priory and this would account for the second part of the name.

SHEEPSTOR - (SX 55 67). Although the connection between the village and the tor close by is obvious, neither has anything to do with sheep - except possibly their droppings! The name of the tor, however, seems to have evolved separately, since it was established as *Shitestorr* by 1291. There were many recorded versions of the village (and parish) name - including *Shistor* (1547); *Shepystor* (1574); and *Shittistor* (1691) with its variant *Shitteslowe*. It has been suggested that all these originate in the Old English *scyttel*, meaning 'bar or bolt' with the suggestion that the tor resembles such an object when viewed from certain vantage points. It has also been suggested that the change from a 't' sound to a 'p' sound might have been a deliberate move away from any lavatorial connotations!

SHILSTONE - (SX 70 90). Shilston(e) itself is an ancient farming community, but the name is a reference to the famous dolmen or cromlech which stands in an adjacent field to the north. The name is compounded from the two Old English words *scylf* - meaning 'shelf', and *stan* meaning 'stone'. Together they define the cromlech with its three granite supports and huge, flat capping stone. There are five other similar place names in Devon, including the Shilstone at Throwleigh (SX 65 90), but no similar remains have been discovered; indeed the surviving one collapsed in 1862 and was restored later the same year. (Maps and signposts refer to the relic as 'Spinsters' Rock(s)', with reference to the legend that three spinster yarn-spinners had raised the monument one morning before breakfast! Of course there must be some doubt as to the type of yarn they used to spin!)

SOUTH BRENT - (SX 69 60). The word Brent is possibly an obscure derivative of the Old English word *brant* meaning 'steep', which would be a reference in this case to the prominent hill of the same name just to the north. The 'South' suggests that there was another settlement of the same name further up the river Avon to the north-west.

STICKLEPATH - (SX 64 94). This ancient village lies tucked in below the great mound of Cosdon Hill. There are several ways up to the moor from here, all of them steep climbs - and that's exactly what 'stickle' means. The original Anglo-Saxon word was *sticol* or *sticele*. The place name was recorded as *Stikelepethe* as early as 1280. The STICKLEPATH in the Walkham valley on the south west edge of the National Park (SX 49 70) is no more than a steep track leading down to Grenofen Bridge from Buckland Monachorum.

THROWLEIGH - (SX 66 90). Situated on the edge of the moor, *Throulegh* was one of the venville 'towns', in other words, a farm that had rights on the moor and surrounding commons. Although the modern spelling is different, the pronounciation is unaltered. The first part of the name is probably derived from the Old English *pruh*, meaning 'chest' or 'coffin', and may refer to the several cains and tumuli (ancient burial mounds) within the parish boundaries. The suffix 'leigh' as usual indicates a clearing.

WALKHAMPTON - (SX 53 69). Certainly this village is situated on the river Walkham, but there has been considerable conjecture amongst writers and historians as to whether the river name was taken from the place name, or vice versa. In his *Guide to Dartmoor* page 126, William Crossing summarises the controversy after noting that part of Walkhampton Common and part of the Chase of Okehampton were both held by the De Redvers family in the 13th century. In this case it would seem appropriate to quote Crossing in full.

> *'It is not a little curious that in the names of these commons the termination "hampton" appears, and yet is found nowhere else on the moor, or in the border parishes. Many of the names of the latter exhibit the oft-found Saxon termination "ton", though in more than one instance the word is apparently traceable to the Celtic "dun", a hill, the heavy sound of the initial letter having given place to a lighter one. But "hampton" is only found in Walkhampton and Okehampton - locally pronounced Wackington and Ockington - though in neither does the word seem to possess its usual signification. It would, however, be unsafe to conclude that it does not."Ham" and "ton" may together, be taken to mean a farm, or enclosed land, with its dwelling-house and outbuildings, the "house town", as it were, and the term came to signify an inhabited settlement. In Walkhampton, the second syllable does not appear to have any connection with the third, but only with the first, the name being derived, we may*

*reasonably suppose, from the river Walkham. Risdon, writing early in
the seventeenth century, calls the river Store, but even if it were
then so known, it is certain that at a much earlier time it bore a
name closely resembling the one by which it is called to-day,
being referred to as the Walkamp in the deed of Isabella de Fortibus.
Thus, Walkhampton would mean the town, or settlement, on the Walkham,
if we could be sure that the deed gave us the earliest form of the
name of the river. But this is doubtful. There are many Dartmoor
streams bearing the name of Walla, or Wella, and one that of Wollake,
and I should be inclined to place Walkham in the same category, and
to regard its early name to have been either Walla or Wollake. In
Saxon times the settlement on the stream would be called
Wallahampton or Wollakhampton, and by an easy transition
Walkhampton. But it is also very probable that we do not see the
word "ham" in this name at all; that the early name of the river
was the Walla, and that Walkhampton is "Walla cwm ton", the town in
the combe, or valley, of the Walla.'*

WALLABROOK - There are several streams on Dartmoor with this name or
known by this name. Whereas the second part, 'brook', has hardly altered in
spelling, pronounciation or meaning from the Old English *broc*, there are several
possibilities as to the origins of 'Walla'. The Anglo-Saxon *waela*, or *wielle* meaning
'well' would do, except that the various streams do not all emerge from distinct
springs, which is what the word implies. Another possibility is that Walla is a
corruption of *walter* meaning 'tumbling' or 'rolling'. Then there's the Anglo-
Saxon word *wileg*, meaning 'willow', and that too could have been the origin.

The Wallabrook (SX 63 87) which is a tributary of the Teign was called
Wotesbrokelakesfote in 1240. If *-oke-* is oak, and *-lake-* is stream, and *-fote* is foot,
then this would refer to the last part of the stream before it joins the main river,
where there are oak trees growing alongside.

The Western Wallabrook (SX 66 67), which is a tributary of the Avon, is spelt
Wellabrook on the Ordnance Survey maps. This variant would be consistent
with the notion that it is a stream distinctly emerging from a spring.

The Hentor Brook (SX 58 65) is sometimes called the Wall or Walla Brook,
but this name is quite separate, since it is a reference to Willings Walls Warren
which is immediately to the south-west.

WARREN HOUSE INN - (SX 67 80) There was no building on this site before 1720, and the present building, erected in 1845, replaced one on the other side of the Moreton to Postbridge road. This was known as Newhouse. The Warren part of the name is a result of its proximity to Headland Warren (see Common Elements). In fact Headland Warren House was at one time an inn (Birch Tor Inn) which was, no doubt, less remote in the days when there was extensive mining in the vicinity! Birch Tor (SX 68 80) was also known as Warren Tor. Leading down from this Tor to Bennet's Cross are a series of bond-stones marked WB for warren boundary. Indeed, the cross itself bears the same inscription, although its history as a route marker and parish boundary stone goes back considerably further. The present Warren House is still comparatively remote - it still has to generate its own electricity - and serves as a welcome rendezvous for the traveller, arriving on foot, horseback or by car.

WIDECOMBE-IN-THE-MOOR - (SX 71 60). All early versions of this name, going back as far as 1270, suggest the name to mean *withy* or 'wide' valley - a suitable name based on obvious physical location. This village, famous for its annual fair, and dominated by ninety feet of church tower, is set in the impressive East Webburn River valley, between Hamel Down to the north-west and Top Tor to the south-east.

Warren House Inn, 1913

WISTMAN'S WOOD - (SX 61 77). Descriptions of this small area of knarled oak trees emerging through moss-covered boulders suggest that it has changed little since the Norman conquest and the subsequent survey of the area - the so-called 'perambulation'. The name is perhaps a reference to the Devil - *wisht* being Devon dialect for 'eerie' or 'uncanny'. Certainly it is a lonely position, up the east side of the West Dart river from Two Bridges, and hugging the side of the valley below Littaford Tors.

Other derivations, however, have been suggested. The Celtic words *visg maen coed* which mean 'stony wood by the water', would make sense phonetically and in meaning. Until quite recently, the old locals spoke of the oak groves as 'Welshman's Wood'. Now this could have been a corruption of *Wealasmans Wood: wealas* meant 'foreigner', and so it could have been the 'Wood of the Celts' who were regarded as foreigners by the Saxon settlers.

The only other similar surviving oak wood is Black-a-Tor Copse(SX 56 89). This is situated on the north-east bank of the West Okement river, in an even more impressive and remote valley bottom - so remote it would seem that even the Ordnance Survey wasn't sure where it was, since, for many years the maps showed the copse as being on the opposite side of the river! (This mistake has more recently been rectified.)

YELVERTON - (SX 52 67). On the east side of Burrator Reservoir (SX 55 68) there is a peninsula on which are the extensive remains of what was obviously an important estate. This was Longstone and the seat of the Elford family from the end of the 15th century to the mid-18th century. The family also possessed property close by Roborough Down and this was called Elford Town. Local dialect gradually changed the pronounciation to Yelver Town or Yelverton, and it was this version that the Great Western Railway Company adopted for the station there, when the branch line from Marsh Mills (Plymouth) to Tavistock was opened in 1859. This is still the name that now describes the main part of the conurbation, but Elfordtown and the nearby farm of the same name, have survived as a separate entity.

Tavistock Turnpike, Two Bridges (SX 60 74)

Books

Baring-Gould, Sabine *A Book of Dartmoor* (Wild Wood House, re-issued 1982 Camelot Press)

Brunsden, D *Dartmoor* (Geographical Association 1968)

Burnard, Robert *Dartmoor Pictorial Records* (Brendon & Son 1890; Devon Books Facsimile Subscriber Edition 1986)

Cocks, John Somers *A Dartmoor Century* (One Hundred Years of the Dartmoor Preservation Association 1883 - 1983) (DPA 1983)

Crossing, William *Princetown - It's Rise and Progress* (Quay Publications 1989) - *Guide to Dartmoor* (Facsimile of the 1912 edition Peninsula Press 1990)

Dartmoor National Park Authority *Dartmoor Place Names Index* (DNPA 1989)

Gover, JEB: Mawer, A: Stenton, FM *The Place Names of Devon, Parts I and II* (English Place Name Society Vol.VIII Cambridge University Press 1931)

Harris, W.Best *Place Names of Plymouth, Dartmoor and the Tamar Valley* (Stannary Press 1987)

Hemery, Eric *High Dartmoor* (Robert Hale 1982) -*Walking the Dartmoor Railroads* (Peninsula Press 1991) - *Walking the Dartmoor Waterways* (Peninsula Press 1991)

Page, John Lloyd Warden *Dartmoor and its Antiquities* (Seeley and Co. 1889)

St Leger-Gordon D *Under Dartmoor Hills* (Robert Hale 1954)

Worth, Hansford *Dartmoor* (Latimer,Trend and Co. 1953)

Index

Abbot's Way Folklore 23; Place Names 10

Arms Tor Tors 29

Ashburton Villages 8,22,24; Tors 9,11,13,14, 26; Place Names 10

Bag Tor Tors 26

barrow see cairne

Baskerville, Hound of the Folklore 9; Tors 28

Beardown Man Place Names 10

Beardown Tors Tors 13,14; Place Names 10

Bel Tor Tors 4, 27

Bellever Folklore 23; Place Names 11

Bellever Forest Folklore 6; Tors 11

Bellever Tor Folklore 28;Tors 11,14

Belstone Villages 12; Folklore 24; Place Names 11

Belstone Common Folklore 20

Bench Tor Tors 9,10

Birch Tor Tors 14; Place Names 29

Birkham Gate Place Names 6

Bittaford Place Names 12

Black Tor Tors 15

Black-a-Tor Copse Place Names 31

Blackingstone Rock Place Names 12

Bonehill Rocks Tors 27

Bovey Tracey Villages 26; Folklore 31; Tors 25,28

Bowerman's Nose Folklore 24; Place Names 12

Brat(Brai) Tor Tors 29

Brent Tor Tors 32; Place Names 12

Buckfast Abbey Folklore 23; Place Names 10,19

Buckfastleigh Folklore 9; Tors 11; Place Names 12

Buckland Abbey Folklore 23

Buckland Beacon Villages 23, Tors 9

Buckland Court Villages 22

Buckland Monachorum Place Names 27

Burrator Reservoir Villages 31; Tors 15; Place Names 6,30

Cadover Bridge Place Names 13

cairne or barrow Tors 17

Castle Arms Inn Villages 20

Castle Drogo Tors 21; Place Names 14

Cator (Common) Folklore 8,9; Place Names 13,19

Chagford Villages 14; Tors 13; Place Names 13

Challacombe Place Names 13

Childe's Tomb Folklore 22; Place Names 13

Chinkwell Tor Tors 27

cist or kistvane Tors 17

clapper bridge Villages 14

clitter Tors 5; Place Names 5

Coombestone Tor Tors 10,11

Cosdon Hill Place Names 14,26

Cox (Cock's) Tor Tors 19,21,32

Cranmere Pool Place Names 14

Crazywell Pool Folklore 21

Crockern Tor Tors 13

Crossing, William Folklore 12,20; Place Names 11,18,19,25,27

Dart Gorge Tors 10

Dart, River Villages 8; Folklore 21; Tors 9; Place Names 5

Dart Valley Villages 22

Dartmeet Folklore 8; Tors 9,10,11; Place Names 5

Dead Lake Place Names 7

Devil's Cauldron Folklore 23

Devil's Pan Tors 22

Devonport Leat Place Names 12

Dewerstone, The Folklore 9,25

Disworthy Warren Place Names 8

Doe Tor Tors 29

Doomsday Book, The Villages 10; Place Names 11,23
Drewe Arms Place Names 15
Drewsteignton Tors 21; Place Names 14
Drift Lane Villages 15
Drizzlecombe Place Names 15
Dunnabridge Pound Tors 11
'Eagle Rock' Tors 10
East Dart Villages 14
East Ockement River Place Names 22
East Webburn River Place Names 29
Erme, River Place Names 15,18
Ermington Place Names 15
Exeter Villages 28; Place Names 20
Fernworthy Place Names 15
Fice's Well Folklore 23
Finch Foundry Museum Villages 28
Fingle Bridge Folklore 18; Place Names 15
Fitz, John Folklore 15,23
Fitzford House Folklore 7,23
Fitz(s) Well(s) Folklore 23; Place Names 8
Foggintor Tors 15,23
Foxtor Mires Folklore 9,22
Freeland Villages 26
Froggymead Place Names 15
Gidleigh Villages 6; Folklore 8,20,30; Place Names 8
Gidleigh Castle Villages 6
Great (Grea) Tor Tors 28
Great Hound Tor Tors 27
Great Links Tor Tors 31
Great Mis Tor Tors 22,32
Great Staple Tor Tors 21,32
Greenhill Villages 28
Grenofen Bridge Place Names 27
Grey Weathers Place Names 18
Grimspound Place Names 18
hairy hands Folklore 6
Hare Tor Tors 31
Harford Place Names 27
Harford Bridge Place Names 18

Hart Hole Lane Folklore 8
Hart Tor Tors 15
Hayne Down Folklore 24
Haytor Tors 25,26
Heath Hounds see Wishthounds
Hentor Brook Place Names 28
Hentor Warren Place Names 8
Hexworthy Villages 9; Tors 9,10; Place Names 18,19
High Willhay Tors 29
Higher White Tor Tors 14
Hill Bridge Place Names 7
Hollow Tor Tors 26
Holne Villages 24; Folklore 18,23; Tors 9,10,11; Place Names 19
Holystreet Folklore 18
Honeybag Tor Tors 27
Horrabridge Place Names 19
Hound Tor Folklore 25; Tors 31
Howard, Lady Folklore 7,9,23
Huccaby Place Names 19
'Jan Coo' Tors 9
Jay's Grave Folklore 14,22
'Jan Reynold's Cards' Tors 14
King's Way Folklore 7
King's Tor Tors 23
Kingsley, Charles Villages 8; Folklore 23
kistvane see cist
Kit's Steps Folklore 23
Kitty Jay see Jay's Grave
Langstone Moor Place Names 7
Laughter Tor Tors11
Launceston Villages 28; Place Names 19
Leeden Tor Tors 15
leat Villages 28; Tors 10
Leather Tor Tors 19
letterboxing Place Names 14
Leusdon Villages 24
Leigh Tor Tors 9
leys Folklore 24

Lich (Lynch) Way Villages 20; Folklore 23; Place Names 7

Littaford Place Names 31

Little Staple Tor Tors 21

logan stone Tors 17,26

Longaford Tor Tors 14

longhouse, Devonshire Villages 18

Lough Tor Tors11

Lower White Tor Tors 14

Lud Brook Place Names 12

Lustleigh Villages 10; Place Names 19

Lustleigh Cleave Villages 10; Place Names 19

Lyd, River Villages 21

Lydford Villages 20; Folklore 7,23; Tors 29,31; Place Names 7,20

Lydford Castle Folklore 23; Tors 13

Lydford Gorge Villages 21; Place Names 20

Manaton Villages 26; Folklore 24; Place Names 20

Marsh Mills Place Names 20

Mary Tavy Tors 31; Place Names 22

Meavy Place Names 20,21

Meavy, River Folklore 25

Mel Tor Tors10

Meldon Place Names 20

menhirs Folklore 20; Tors 11,17; Place Names 15

Merripit Hill Folklore 8

Merrivale Tors 21,22; Place Names 22

Metherall Place Names 15

Middle Staple Tor Tors 21

Moorgate Villages 19

Moretonhampstead Villages 10,14,18,26; Folklore 9,30,31; Tors11,13,28; Place Names 22,23

Mount, The Villages 28

New Bridge Villages 24; Folklore 18; Tors 9,10

Nine Maidens, The Folklore 12,20

North Bovey Villages 18; Folklore 11

North Hessary Tor Tors 15,23; Place Names 8

Nun's Cross see Siward's Cross

O'brook stream Tors 11

Okehampton Villages 12,28; Folklore 23; Tors 29,31; Place Names 14,22

Okehampton Castle Folklore 7,8,9

Okement Place Names 22

Oxenham, 'Lady' Margaret Folklore 7

Peak Hill Tors 19

Peter Tavy Place Names 23

Petticoat Lane Folklore 8

Phillpotts, Eden Folklore 20

Pil Tor Tors 26

Pixies Folklore 14

Pixies' Cave, Cross, Holt, Parlour Folklore 18; **House** Folklore 18; Tors 19

Pizwell Folklore 9

Plym, River Folklore 25; Place Names 12

Plymouth Place Names 10,12,19; Tors 19

Postbridge Tors 11,14; Place Names 22,29

pound Tors 11,17

Poundsgate Villages 24; Tors 10

Prince Hall Place Names 24

Princetown Villages 14; Folklore 9,21,23; Tors 15,23; Place Names 8,13,24

Puggie Stone, The Folklore 18

Ramsley Villages 28

Raven Tor Tors 26

Red Lake Place Names 7

Rippon Tor Tors 25

Roborough Down Folklore 21

rock basins Tors 17,22

Roos Tor Tors 21,32

Ruddycleave Villages 22

Rundlestone/Rundle Stone Place Names 25

Rundlestone Tor Place Names 25

Saddle Tor Tors 25

Sampford Spiney Place Names 25

Sandy Ford Place Names 6,7

Sandy Park Folklore 18

Scorhill Folklore 20

Sharp Tor Tors 6,9,10,31

Sharp Tor Tors 6,9,10,31
Sharpitor Tors 19
Shaugh Prior Place Names 25
Sheeps Tor Tors 19
Sheepstor Villages 31; Folklore 18,21;
  Place Names 26
Shilstone Place Names 26
Sittaford Tor Place Names 18
Siward's (or Nun's) Cross Place Names 10,25
Skerraton Place Names 6
Sourton Tors Tors 29
South Brent Place Names 26
South Hams Place Names 7
South Hessary Tor Tors 19
South Tawton Folklore 6
South Teign Place Names 15
Spinsters' Rock Folklore 24; Place Names 26
Spitchwick Villages 24; Tors 9
standing stones see menhirs
stannary courts, towns Tors 13;
  Place Names 8,10,13
Stannon House Villages 14
Sticklepath Villages 28; Place Names 26
Swell Tor Tors 15,23,
Tavistock Villages 14,20; Folklore 7,14,30;
  Tors 13,15,21,29,32;
  Place Names 7,8,10,18,25
Tavistock Inn Villages 24
Tavy Cleave Tors 31; Place Names 6
Tavy, River Tors 32; Place Names 7,18,32
Taw, River Villages 28
Teign, River Folklore 18;
  Place Names 13,14,15,28
'Ten Commandments, The' Villages 23;
  Tors 9
Throwleigh Folklore 8; Place Names 26,27
Top Tor Tors 26; Place Names 29
Tor Abbey Villages 22
Tor Royal Place Names 24
Town Orchard Villages 10

Two Bridges Villages 24; Folklore 6;
  Tors 11,13,15,21,23,32;
  Place Names 24,25,31
Ugborough Beacon Place Names 5
Venford Villages 9
Venford Reservoir Tors 10
Vixana Folklore 11
Vixen Tor Folklore 11; Tors 21,22
Walkham, River Place Names 19,27
Walkhampton Place Names 25,27
Wallabrook Place Names 28
Wallabrook Bridge Folklore 8
Warren House Inn Tors 14; Place Names 29
Water Villages 26
Webburn Villages 22,24
West Dart Tors 14; Place Names 19,31
West Ockement Place Names 22,31
Wheal Betsy Tors 32; Place Names 9
White Barrow Place Names 7
White Bird of the Oxenhams Folklore 6
White Tor Tors 32
Widecombe (-in-the-Moor) Villages 24;
  Folklore 11,20,30; Tors 9,14,25,26,28;
  Place Names 13,29
Wish (Wisht) Hounds Folklore 8;
  Place Names 30
Wistman's Wood Folklore 9;
  Place Names 5,10,30
witches/witchcraft Folklore 11,20
Wreyland Villages 11
Yar Tor Tors 10
Yelverton Villages 31; Tors 15,19,23;
  Place Names 30
Yennadon Down Place Names 13
Yes Tor Tors 29
Yeth Hounds see Wisht Hounds